THE
KEY
to
YOUR
ENERGY

THE
KEY
to
YOUR
ENERGY

22 Steps to Rebuild Your Energy
and Free Yourself Emotionally

NATACHA CALESTRÉMÉ

 sourcebooks

Published by Sourcebooks
P.O. Box 4410, Naperville, Illinois 60567-4410
(630) 961-3900
sourcebooks.com

First published in French as *La Clé de votre énergie: 22 protocoles pour
vous libérer émotionnellement* by Éditions Albin Michel in 2020

This edition originally published in 2023 in Great Britain by
Vermilion, an imprint of Ebury Publishing. Vermilion is part
of the Penguin Random House group of companies whose
addresses can be found at global.penguinrandomhouse.com

Cataloging-in-Publication Data is on file with the Library of Congress.

Printed and bound in the United States of America.
POD 10 9 8 7 6 5 4 3 2 1

Contents

Part Three: Your Emotional Health Check

Introduction

We've all experienced ordeals in our lives, and we all hope that one day we'll recover from the effects. Bereavement, break-ups, illness, failure, redundancy, family difficulties . . . sometimes life just seems to have it in for us. We pick ourselves up after one blow, only for the next one to send us tumbling straight down again.

We've tried switching to organic food, we've meditated, and we've seen therapists who tell us how to love and forgive ourselves. It's true that those things help lessen the urge to run away to a desert island, but our feelings of anger and frustration still rise up more strongly with every new difficulty, and we can't help thinking, *I'm doing everything I should! Why does it never work?*

So what's the answer? How can we feel better, rebuild ourselves, and rediscover joy and serenity? While I still had a little bit of energy, my optimism would carry me through, and I'd keep postponing the day when I'd seek an answer to these vital questions. I could always find a good reason to keep going. Like a workhorse, I exhausted myself dragging emotional burdens that only grew heavier as the years went on. At the time I wasn't aware of my own suffering, until the terrible day when my body gave in: I began to suffer awful pain that began in my back and spread right down my legs, so I could no longer sit, stand or lie down comfortably. I was soon diagnosed with double slipped discs. Not something that would kill me, admittedly; but, for a creature used to living life at a permanent gallop, this agonising immobility felt like a disaster.

Pretending I was fine had now become impossible and, as I could no longer move, I forced myself to take stock. Life had given me some hard knocks over the previous four years. The repercussions of my divorce from my first husband were still having a painful impact on my family. I'd lost confidence in myself professionally after having a book manuscript and a few documentary projects rejected. And then tragedy had struck: my younger sister, to whom I'd grown very close in the last three years, had died after spending several months in a coma. A short while later, one of my friends died from the effects of her husband's long-term abuse. Then came a more trivial incident, but one that proved to be the final straw: I was unexpectedly verbally abused by an acquaintance I'd hurt without realising it. Two days later, I was paralysed by the double slipped discs. Despite the caring presence of my husband, Stéphane, I was crying with pain, frightened by the brutality of what my body was putting me through. No need to read Freud to conclude that it wasn't just this latest incident that had brought me down, but the accumulation of all my difficulties. I was a snail stranded in the hot sun, and my shell was cracked. Mending myself had to be my priority now.

I became an avid reader of personal development books, hoping to find the key that would help me escape from my state of distress. I was especially attracted by the writing of the psychiatrist Carl Gustav Jung, founder of analytical psychology: 'Those who learn nothing from the unpleasant incidents in their lives force the cosmic consciousness to repeat them as many times as necessary for the lesson taught by the incident to be learned.

What you deny subjugates you. What you accept transforms you.' In other words, as long as our emotional injuries are not healed, the universe – what Jung calls the *cosmic consciousness* – will ensure that we attract people and situations that make us relive these injuries, in order to give us a chance to understand their meaning, take control of them, and stop them affecting us.

Time went by, but this idea of Jung's lingered in my mind. In the meantime, something serious was happening in my professional life. I'd spent the last fifteen years making wildlife documentaries and conducting scientific studies, moving straight from one film project to the next, but for a year now every single one of my projects had been rejected by all the television stations. Incomprehension gave way to frustration. I told myself that something would eventually be accepted, but months passed and nothing happened. I found myself out of work. With unemployment came a sense of shame, then the end of my benefits, then no more money. I was broke.

Things carried on like this until one day I was called for a meeting at the employment agency to assess my progress in looking for work. I took it as an attack. 'Everything's fine, I'm writing my next novel, I've got some film projects on the go, you don't need to summon me, I won't come,' I replied, with all the diplomacy of an angry bulldog. But they weren't interested in my tantrums, and a few weeks later I found myself in Saint-Denis at the branch of the agency specialising in the creative industries. Once I was there, I ended up relaxing a little, and even built up a rapport with the friendly advisor. I told her about my various projects, and about my dream to write a script for a television series. After a two-hour meeting, I got up to say goodbye. 'You haven't left me your email address,' she reminded me. I explained that I preferred to keep it private, to avoid being deluged by useless messages. 'That's a shame, because you could register for updates about training courses,' she replied. Ignoring my objections, she scrolled through a few pages on her screen, then said: 'Look, we've had a message about a masterclass run by the Luc Besson film school.' I sat down again, intrigued. She held out a bunch of leaflets describing different courses. I took one at random and read: 'Learn how to write a television series.' My jaw dropped and my heart began to race. Immediately, that message of Jung's sprang to my mind: *Learn something from your difficulties.*' If there'd been no rejections from television stations, there'd have been no unemployment, no meeting, no chance of hearing about this course. Could it be that this lack of work, which I perceived as an injustice, would actually be the key to fulfilling my dream?

Having read the small print, I learned that the masterclass was expensive, and began in just three weeks. I didn't have a minute to lose. I thanked the advisor and rushed off to put together my application for funding for the course. When I arrived, trembling, at the funding body's offices, I presented myself at the counter, only to be disappointed. 'I'm sorry,' said the receptionist, handing back my application, 'the deadline is always a month before the course, but yours starts in three weeks, so it's too late.' My head was spinning, torn between doubt and certainty. But if Jung was right, I was meant to take this course.

'There must be a solution,' I said, hesitantly. I had a feeling that what happened now would have an impact on all the difficulties in my life. If I could enrol, I'd put everything I had into 'learning the lessons' from the painful events in my past.

'You're not an author, by any chance?' she asked.

'Yes, I am . . .'

'Because if you can prove you earned at least 9,000 euros over the last two years as a writer or a scriptwriter, that's

OK – the deadline for authors is three weeks instead of a month, and it's today.'

I hurried home to put together the documents I needed. It wasn't long before the good news came: my funding application had been successful. A week later, I was called for an interview at the film school, and was offered one of the eight available places. I couldn't believe what had just happened!

I didn't know it at the time, but the story didn't end there. A few months later, one of the teachers on the course left and the director of the school, who was familiar with my work as a novelist, asked me to teach a course on 'Writing a Script and Creating a Character' to first- and second-year students. The cherry on the cake was that a producer later asked me to write the script for a new television series.

There was only one conclusion to be drawn: the unemployment that had felt like a disaster was actually the first step towards fulfilling my dream.

That day I understood that everything had meaning.

What next? What could I do to heal myself and move forward? Years earlier, working as a journalist and director, I'd met people who'd suggested that I should think differently about the wounds that life could inflict. At the time it hadn't seemed relevant to me, but my Cartesian view of the world, with its clear distinctions between the mental and the physical, had been called into question. Healers, hypnotists, mediums and shamans: they had all described their healing techniques, and had told me how they had learned to pick themselves up after a knock. It was neither biology nor psychology, but an energy and a vision that were profoundly different from everything I'd been taught up until then. Could it help me now?

I applied the techniques. Week after week, month after month, I rebuilt myself by freeing myself from the wounds inherited from my family, seeing off my fears, shedding my guilt and healing myself. My life was transformed and enhanced.

I then decided to share these re-energising techniques in workshops, and what a pleasure it was to bring together therapists, psychologists and even doctors from all over the country. During these years I received so much feedback from strangers whose lives had been changed that I had a lightbulb moment: it was time to share this precious knowledge. This book is the fruit of a ten-year journey. It will help you to free yourself from your painful emotions and reconnect with your inner strength, the key to your energy.

Tip: You can try all the techniques one after another, or you can pick only those that feel relevant to you, but it's vital to take the time to read the whole book before acting on techniques 5 and 6. If you were simply to skip to those points without reading what comes before, you wouldn't be aware of the precautions and explanations needed, and that could result in failure. **Give yourself the chance to succeed** by absorbing the message of the whole book.

PART ONE

Find the Right Diagnosis!

Chapter 1

Identifying Emotional Injuries

C hanging how we react to adversity: that's our goal. Something wonderful can be concealed within the most difficult experiences. At first we only see mud, but soon we understand that it's actually fertiliser, which will help us to grow in a different way. By taking a step back from events, we can stop seeing them as catastrophes, and every difficulty can become an experience. We are not victims of fate, and nor are we being unfairly targeted: there is something positive to be gained from what we are going through.

I gradually became more receptive to this approach, and soon discovered Lise Bourbeau's bestseller, *Heal Your Wounds and Find Your True Self.** Bourbeau is a Canadian therapist whose research is based on the work of Sigmund Freud, the founder of psychoanalysis. Freud says that our physical appearance may have something to tell us about our emotions. Having studied thousands of cases, Bourbeau suggests that there are five wounds, which may also be linked to physical characteristics: rejection, abandonment, humiliation, betrayal and injustice.†

Every one of us will experience two of three of these more

---

* Lotus Press, 2002.

† There are five more wounds: anger, powerlessness, sadness, guilt and fear. These are not covered by Bourbeau in her books, but they are just as important. I examine them in *Trouver ma place: 22 protocoles pour*

than the others. Bourbeau describes how our bodies bear the signs of each wound, and provides a sketch of the effects of each one. I have chosen to describe their key characteristics by relating them to well-known people.

The Five Main Wounds

Rejection: Slim or narrow body in childhood that may broaden with age, often with a hollow chest. Seeks perfection in work, values solitude, is seen as someone who 'keeps themself to themself' at work, and prefers to give up when faced with a difficult situation rather than going into battle.

Abandonment: Body lacking tone, curved back, sad expression, seeks attention and blossoms in a career that offers public visibility. Asks for advice but does not always follow it, dislikes living alone, behaves warmly to those around them.

Humiliation: Round face and body, wide eyes, likes to take their time, does everything possible to avoid criticism; generous, feels obliged to do more for others than for themself, and sometimes feels exploited.

Betrayal: Well-proportioned body, demonstrates strength and power, an intense and seductive expression, does not see other people's problems as a priority, likes to control every situation and do everything independently, seeks to impress people, understands and acts quickly in new situations.

---

accéder au bonheur (Finding My Place: 22 Steps to Achieving Happiness) (Albin Michel, 2021).

Injustice: Upright, 'perfect' body, round buttocks, lively expression, makes a lot of demands of themselves, perfectionist. Feels as though there's nothing wrong, and finds it difficult to enjoy things without feeling guilty.

Becoming aware of our wounds is an interesting process because it alerts us to scenarios in our lives that might be repeating themselves. If you find it difficult to identify the two or three wounds that best represent you, don't worry, just carry on reading. There are other ways of achieving emotional freedom.

If your reaction to what you've just read is: 'I don't see myself in any of those!', but your friends say: 'But that one is an exact description of you!' – that's normal! Our minds always try to keep our wounds at a distance, in order to protect us from such painful knowledge. I saw this for myself at a conference when I'd just described the five wounds. A man came over to me and said: 'I've noted down four wounds, but I missed one.' I pointed out that the one he'd missed was almost certainly his main wound, and that his mind was trying to protect him in case he wasn't ready to face the reality. He smiled incredulously at me. I asked him to tell me which wounds he'd noted down, and betrayal was the only one missing. 'That's the story of my life,' he murmured, astonished.

Are you ready to give it a try? Note down the five wounds without looking back at the previous page. The point isn't to test your memory but to do an experiment.

1 _____

2 _____

3 _____

4 _____

5 _____

If you forget one or two, you're in luck: you've almost certainly identified your main wounds. If not, use the physical descriptions, not forgetting that we all have more than one wound and are therefore a complex blend of several of them.

> *The way our bodies express our main wounds is very interesting, but more surprising is what Lise Bourbeau says about the origin of these wounds: 'Our souls seem to choose a certain number of wounds to experience, for example, rejection and injustice, or betrayal and abandonment. Once they are defined, we constantly attract people and situations that make us re-live these wounds, until they cease to have an impact on us.'*

It would seem that the first people we *choose* are our parents. Our soul decides on the social, cultural and family *environment* in which we will be born. When I discovered this, I was confused; but then I made the television series *Enquêtes extraordinaires* (*Extraordinary Investigations*), examining the theory of the persistence of consciousness after death, and everything I believed was called into question. A little over half of the world's population believes in reincarnation, but it still seemed to me a distant and improbable notion. I could never have imagined what I would discover when I studied the story of little James Leininger, a very well-documented case that remains a mystery to science.

James was born in Louisiana, and in the year 2000, when he was two, he began to have nightmares. He would cry out, 'Plane on fire!' and beat his hands on the bars of his cot, shouting that he couldn't get out of the cockpit. As he grew older, he said he was an American pilot who'd served during the Second World War, based on the aircraft carrier the USS *Natoma Bay*. He even gave the names of his crew, and identified the island of Iwo Jima as the place where his plane had been shot down. It would take ten years of research before his parents, who were very sceptical, would admit that he must be the reincarnation of James Huston, killed in 1945 by the Japanese army during an air raid. All the details given by the child, many of which had been kept confidential by the army, were checked in 2011 and found to be correct. All this is astonishing, but perhaps the most striking thing is what James said to his parents about his conception: 'I chose you, you and Mommy, to be my parents.' His father, amazed, asked him when he had made this choice. 'When you were on holiday in Hawaii, in the pink hotel.' James had indeed been conceived on a holiday to the Pink Palace Hotel in Hawaii!

As bizarre as it may seem, we do apparently choose our parents. And not just them, but all of our circle of family, friends and colleagues. As the Dalai Lama says: 'There are more than 8 billion of us on Earth; it's not possible that the people close to us are there by accident.'

But what can we do to prevent our emotional wounds recurring?

Chapter 2

Breaking the Cycle of Emotional Wounds

The first step is becoming aware of your wounds and **accepting** them. If you didn't identify your main wounds in the previous exercise, and you didn't recognise yourself in the physical descriptions, here's a different method: write down the key words that remind you of six ordeals you have been through. For example, it could be the name of somebody who left you or cheated on you, a bereavement that left you devastated, a slap that you were given as a child, an upsetting comment by a family member or colleague, a car accident, a disagreement, the loss of a pet, a job you didn't get ... Feel free to include anything, noting down whatever springs to mind, whether it's recent or in the past. The more difficulties we recall, the more revealing the next stage will be.

- _____

- _____

- _____

- _____

- _____

- _____

Identifying the Ordeal

The next step is to match each ordeal with a letter, depending on how you experienced each one: I for injustice, R for rejection, A for abandonment, B for betrayal, H for humiliation. If one ordeal involves two wounds (for example, injustice and betrayal), note down both corresponding letters. It's often difficult to distinguish between rejection and abandonment: rejection is the result of a decision (for example, as a child we were told, 'You can't eat until you've finished your homework') whereas abandonment is due to neglect or an event that is *seemingly independent* of our own will (for example, 'I'm late to collect you because there was a traffic jam').

Count up the number of times each letter occurs. If two or three wounds recur more than the others, and that confirms what you already thought, that's great! Or are you surprised by the result? Even better! Either way, you have just identified the wounds that are having an impact on your life. Remember that each ordeal can be perceived differently depending on the person experiencing it. A break-up can be seen as abandonment by one person, or as rejection, betrayal, humiliation or injustice by another. Similarly, losing a job, being cheated on, failing at something or having an accident – events that are unrelated to one another – can all be experienced as (for example) injustice.

This exercise has enabled you to identify the wounds that feed the cycle of ordeals described by Jung. We have all met people going through these kinds of difficulties:

'It's awful, all the women I go out with cheat on me . . .'

'I'm in a mess, all my managers are angry with me . . .'

'It's unbelievable, every time I buy a new car, there's a problem with it . . .'

- *If we see these ordeals as disasters or strokes of bad luck, putting the blame on others and positioning ourselves as victims, we're missing the point. Our soul has chosen to test out certain wounds, and we have to work through them to stop them having an impact on us. This is our **principal challenge**.*

- *If this ordeal endlessly repeats itself in a vicious cycle, it means we've missed the vital message: one of our old wounds has not healed yet. A painful experience always hides a 'gift' that is invisible until some time afterwards: it gives us the opportunity to rebuild ourselves, having gained increased awareness of this fault line inside us.*

- *Astonishingly, we will come to realise that we are making ourselves and those around us relive this same ordeal endlessly. The best way to prevent this wound from affecting us is to stop making ourselves and others experience it again and again.*

The examples of famous people will help us to understand the boomerang effect of emotional wounds, and the vicious cycle they can initiate.

Rejection

Andy Warhol was one of the greatest artists of the twentieth century, and yet as a student he felt *rejected* and disliked, and his work was always controversial among his peers. Warhol was obsessed with death, prone to anorexia (a form of *rejection* of one's own body), and extremely perfectionist, carrying the wound of rejection. This type of personality, although world famous, remains 'apart', excelling in their field but keeping their distance from other people.

In order to move beyond the wound of rejection, we must stop inflicting it on ourselves and others. We must stop running away from the problem by moving house, stop avoiding people who annoy us, choose occupations that don't entail making choices (accountancy, research, analysis, administrative work, etc.), and be measured in our assessments of other people's behaviour (especially if our work entails judging others). Healing ourselves means no longer making others experience our rejection.

Abandonment

Woody Allen has a sad expression despite his exceptional sense of humour. Exaggerating his hunched posture and lethargic demeanour, Allen, the king of self-mockery, constantly casts himself at the centre of his films. This craving for attention is common among artists of all kinds, and is typical of the wound of abandonment. King Charles III was four when his mother *abandoned* him by ceasing to prioritise her role as a mother and becoming Queen. For him, as for all those bearing this wound, single life is unthinkable. He *abandoned* Camilla Parker Bowles for Princess Diana, and then *abandoned* Diana to return to Camilla.

By putting an end to our dependence on the judgement of others, we can free ourselves from the wound of abandonment, but we must also take care not to *abandon* our friends or those around us at the first sign of disagreement, and avoid *abandoning* our projects (passion, hobbies or professional projects).

Humiliation

The former British prime minister Margaret Thatcher was known for her biting, even humiliating, put-downs, so much so that she became known as the 'Iron Lady'. The same was true of the former French president François Mitterrand, whose barbed comments were infamous. Marlon Brando, who was a bulky man (a typical characteristic of humiliation), was ashamed of his mother's alcoholism, and the fact that she often ended her evenings passed out in a bar. Having been *humiliated* as a child, he relived this wound when his stream of film roles began to dry up, and he carried on *humiliating* himself in later life by not maintaining his appearance: he weighed 136 kilos by the time he died.

If we no longer want to be on the receiving end of unpleasant comments from our personal and professional acquaintances, or even from strangers on the street, it's important that we avoid making fun of others with humiliating remarks or belittling nicknames. If we resist the temptation to make one too many mocking observations (in an effort not to disappoint our audience) we will feel less mocked by others. When we pay careful attention to the way we treat ourselves ('I'm stupid') and the way we eat, this wound of humiliation can be healed.

Betrayal

Extrovert, impatient, seductive and full of confidence: those who carry the wound of betrayal have a talent for comedy, politics and strategy.

We need to stop wanting to control everything and everyone around us – to help them, we tell ourselves, but actually to reassure ourselves. Fulfilling our duty to ourselves (diet, exercise, relaxation, giving up smoking, etc.) is the first step along the path to freeing ourselves from the wound of betrayal. If we can learn to be less impatient, if we can rid ourselves of the conviction that we hold the key to the truth about everything, then betrayal, whether personal or professional, will only be a distant memory.

Injustice

Zinedine Zidane, one of the greatest footballers in the world, is famous for his sporting genius and footwork but also for the terrible incident that occurred during the 2006 World Cup final. What an *injustice* for a player at that level! After being on the receiving end of a string of insults about his family, Zidane headbutted the Italian player who was abusing him *unjustly*. He was sent off and made his team suffer the *injustice* of losing the trophy. Similarly, John F. Kennedy, the youngest ever American president, had an upright posture, round buttocks and a seemingly impeccable demeanour (the main characteristics of injustice), and his family suffered a series of *unjust* tragedies.

How can we stop feeling as though we're being treated *unjustly*? First of all by becoming aware of the injustice we're committing against ourselves, such as endlessly seeking perfection in every area of our lives instead of looking after our health or spending time with our families. We can begin by opening our eyes to our own moods and acknowledging what brings us pleasure, in order to avoid burnout. We can also make sure we don't forget *unjustly* about all those who have helped us, and reflect on the wider impact of all our decisions.

*

It is often the case that we bear the marks of two main wounds, which makes them difficult to identify. We may have a perfectly proportioned body (the wound of injustice) with hips slightly wider than the shoulders (the wound of betrayal) and we will find ourselves experiencing both. Similarly, if we tend to put on weight easily and our body lacks tone, it can mean that we are carrying the wounds of abandonment and humiliation.

Acknowledging the Ordeal

Whether we carry one or several wounds, the key is to be aware of what we are forcing ourselves and those around us to undergo, and to observe the way we perceive events in our lives. The following example is a clear illustration of this. Nicole took part in one of my workshops, and she told me about her feeling of injustice when her partner didn't wish her a happy birthday as soon as she woke up. (Others might have experienced this as rejection, betrayal, humiliation or abandonment, depending on their wounds.) That evening, she discovered that he had organised a surprise party for her with all her friends, and she felt the same sense of injustice, but this time because he hadn't guessed that she would have preferred a romantic dinner. With hindsight, she realised that she had viewed events through the lens of her wound. She hadn't been able to see that she was also inflicting injustice upon others by complaining about everything, even though her partner had been thinking of her all along.

Throughout our lives, we will be drawn to people and situations that give us the opportunity to relive these wounds in order to heal them. Understanding this allows us to avoid hasty judgements about those around us, and to develop more effective reactions to such situations.

From now on, we must see every new obstacle as an opportunity to correct our attitude. Here is an example: Laurent, a friend who lives in south-west France, owns an apartment in Paris that he shares with his sister, who lives in Spain. He carries the wound of rejection, and treasures his moments of solitude, hating having his space invaded by strangers. Because *we attract situations that make us relive our wounds*, it happened by *chance* that his sister told some friends of hers that they could stay in the flat while Laurent was there. He experienced this interruption as a rejection by his sister, and rejected her in his turn by banning any unexpected visits in the future. Until, that is, the day when his sister's mother-in-law, who had cancer, needed to come to Paris for some scans during a week when Laurent was in the flat. He was stubborn: 'She can come, but I'll go and stay in a hotel.' He was rejecting her. Laurent shifted the problem by removing himself from the apartment. He hadn't understood that circumstances were *conspiring* to place him face-to-face with his wound as many times as necessary, until he learned from the situation: he must stop forcing others to experience rejection. On my advice, he decided to welcome his sister's mother-in-law to the apartment, and to stay there himself. What happened? She wrote to him to explain that she had arranged to stay with a friend for emotional support, so in the end Laurent was not troubled by her presence.

- If we can stop making ourselves and those around us relive our wounds, we will stop the same ordeals recurring throughout our lives. Breaking off our relationship with the person who reactivates our wound is not the solution.

Recognising our wound, accepting it, and becoming aware of its cycles and what it RE-presents for our wellbeing is the best way of curing it and ending our suffering.

- *Recognising our wound doesn't mean accepting everything that happens to us. If we are subjected to abuse, psychological aggression, or simply unkind words, it is vital that we protect ourselves and express our feelings. Of course, I'm not talking here about rape, or any form of sexual aggression or physical violence: in these cases, escape is the only option. After we have reacted to the situation, it is the ordeal itself that we must see as a learning opportunity. With hindsight, sometimes many years later, when we have rebuilt ourselves and, perhaps, forgiven the person in question, we will have grown stronger, and developed skills and talents that we had never imagined possible. Then, the time will have come to look back at the ordeal with different eyes.*

Meanwhile, as we progress towards feeling better, we have the right to share our distress and anger. It's normal to resent somebody for what they have put us through, even if that person is our parent, brother, sister, grandparent, spouse or friend. But in order to accept the ordeal and progress along our path in life, it is wise to free ourselves of our toxic emotion. One day, we will manage it. Everything comes with time.

I advise you to banish your resentment, your bitterness, your frustration and your anger – by going for a walk and having a good shout, if you like, or better yet by talking to someone you know or to a therapist. That way, these feelings will not express themselves through violence or illness. If you can't manage to take a step back now, the next chapters will help you. And don't forget: the people who cause our suffering also help us to become aware of our wounds and their vicious cycles, and to rid ourselves of them, even if that might seem hard to believe. Our torturers suddenly become our best allies in our future development.

Taking a Step Back from the Ordeal

Sometimes we choose the wrong target. When that happens, it's a sure sign that we're blaming ourselves for something. For example, if our father has caused us serious harm, but some unconscious force makes us resent our mother more for not having defended us, it often means that we actually blame ourselves for not having known how to say 'stop'. Similarly, if a friend makes a decision that we find hurtful, and our anger focuses instead on his wife, because 'it's always her fault', it means that we are angry with ourselves for not having foreseen the problem with our friend. And, to give one final example, if we're being harassed at work and criticise our brother for not caring, it's often a sign that we blame ourselves for not managing to stand up to our boss.

This concealed resentment causes us to harm ourselves mentally and physically: we are punishing ourselves. This takes on a very physical form when we accidentally trip on the stairs, bang our head *stupidly*, or stub our toe. These physical knocks are the expression of our guilt.

The more we have suffered, the more our minds prevent us from seeing the truth. Those readers who are sceptical of that idea are the ones who have undergone especially difficult experiences. In a bid to protect us, our minds prevent us from understanding.

TECHNIQUE 1

Breaking the cycle of emotional wounds

1. Become aware of the repetitive cycles in order to identify the wounds that are affecting you (rejection, abandonment, humiliation, injustice or betrayal).

   Note: If you feel certain that you are not affected by any wounds, it's a sign that you are carrying the wound of injustice, which causes you to say, *unjustly*: 'There's nothing wrong, I'm fine.' In fact, this wound often leads to burnout, because being unaware of your suffering means you never stop working.

2. Realise that the person causing you pain is likely to have the same wound as you, and that they are helping you to become familiar with your vulnerable points.

3. Set boundaries, marking out what you find acceptable, and confide your feelings to others in order to free yourself from anger. Tell the person in question that they have caused you to relive a wound. Make sure you don't make those around you relive the same wound.

4. Stop inflicting the wound on yourself.

5. Moving beyond this difficulty means understanding that it is constantly drawing you back to something that needs to be healed. It means breaking the repetitive cycle.

6. No longer feeling resentful of the person who has hurt us is the first step towards healing our wound.

7. Don't do all this for somebody else's sake: do it because it's the only way to free yourself.

8. When a wound no longer repeats itself, it means that you have successfully healed it.

Chapter 3

Understanding the Meaning
of Illness

The first time I ever thought of my health as something other than a purely medical affair was when I had a raging fever that kept me in bed for two days. I went to the doctor, naturally. As I was getting up to leave, he saw me grimace as I pulled my coat on. I hadn't told him about a pain in my **shoulder** that shot through me every time I moved. 'Who've you got it in for?' he asked, with a smile. I didn't understand his question straight away. I couldn't see how it related to my fever, still less to the pain that was dogging me. He explained that several of his patients suffering from shoulder pain had one thing in common: a desire to lash out at someone they knew. It was a desire I shared. Do our personal relationships have an impact on our health? My doctor recommended that I work on my relationship with the person who was, at that point, dominating my thoughts. The second step was to see a psychotherapist once a week for almost a year. Unbelievable as it may seem, the pain gradually eased and eventually disappeared, without the help of any medication whatsoever. At the time I didn't understand the forces at work, but I remembered this episode when I had my slipped discs. The solution was now clear: it was possible to heal first by consulting a doctor and then by thinking *differently* about the origin of our illness.

The Cycle of Illness

Of all the cycles that repeat themselves during our lives, illness recurs most frequently. Unfortunately, we tend not to pay enough attention to this recurrence; or worse, we even become used to falling ill. Throat infections, colds, bugs, migraines, constipation, inflammation, asthma, backache, cystitis . . . Could it be that when these illnesses recur, it's not simply bad luck? Could it be that, as with difficulties in life, this vicious cycle has a meaning? When we're ill and stuck in bed, we think we're vulnerable to certain microbes and bacteria, or that we've caught a nasty virus that's going round. Cold weather, outbreaks of certain illnesses, or even inherited predisposition: all these factors cause us to fall ill. And family doctors often observe that many of their patients' illnesses recur. It's hard not to feel helpless knowing that although medicine can usually treat the worst effects of the illness, it doesn't stop it coming back. What can we do to avoid this?

Through analysis of our different reactions to illness, I have observed that we often have a careless attitude towards our bodies. Let's take the example of headaches, one of the most common sources of pain. Usually, our first reaction is to say, 'It's fine, it'll go away by itself.' Then, if the pain persists, we take a painkiller. We could compare this situation to driving a car when the red light signalling brake problems comes on. If we reacted in the same way, thinking, 'It'll go away by itself,' we wouldn't change the brake pads and would drive straight into an accident. As for the second stage, when we take a painkiller that dulls the pain without treating the cause, it's as though we've simply switched off the red warning light. That wouldn't stop us driving into a wall because the brakes would still be faulty and, in this example, we are the car!

This comparison demonstrates two things: first, that we look after our cars better than we look after our bodies (we change the brake pads but, when it comes to ourselves, we just remove the symptom); second, that we worry more about the effects of a problem than its origins.

The remedies available – whether chemical or plant-based – do no more than *switch off the little red light* by removing the symptoms. For example, if I catch a bacterial throat infection, I'll be given antibiotics; if my back is stiff, I'll be prescribed a muscle relaxant; if I have eczema, the doctor will recommend hydrocortisone; if I suffer from panic attacks, I'll get tranquilisers. But do all these drugs really combat the cause of the problem? No. The proof is that the illness keeps coming back. How many people suffering from inflammation in their right foot have taken a course of anti-inflammatories and had the pain disappear, only to find it reappearing in the left foot?

Viruses, microbes, and bacteria have existed on Earth for millions of years. Over time, they have evolved and adapted to changes in our planet and its inhabitants. If the mere presence of pathogens were enough to make us fall ill, we'd all be ill all the time. However, some of us fall ill while others remain healthy. Another anomaly: viruses need heat in order to reproduce, but they do the most damage in winter. Might our bodies sometimes grow so weak that they are vulnerable to the carriers of these pathologies?

Other theories suggest that illness arises from an imbalance within the body. Biological analysis would seem to confirm this: a lack of magnesium is linked to stress, excessive iron in the body can cause neurological problems, 'bad' cholesterol leads to poor circulation, and a proliferation of certain bacteria can cause a urine infection. Now let's reverse the causal link. What if the fluctuations in these molecules were actually a consequence of the body's weakness? That would explain why most of us are *healthy* carriers of substances that are potentially pathogenic, and only a small minority of us will suffer the illness. The human papillomavirus is a clear illustration. In France, 85 per cent of women are exposed to this virus at some time or another, and yet only 0.002 per cent of them will develop cervical cancer. So why will only about 527 people be affected, instead of all the 31 million women who have been exposed? The presence of the virus in the blood doesn't necessarily result in illness, so why do some women fall ill? Again, we can suggest the same hypothesis: a weakened body.

Another cause of recurrent illness is our diet. If it is too high in fat or sugar, not only do we become prone to indigestion, but we also risk becoming overweight or even diabetic. In this case, excess seems to be the aggravating factor. But why do some of us eat more than we need? Is there a gap we are trying to fill by eating excessively? Might our bodies be trying to compensate for their weakness by seeking energy where they know they will find it: in sugar, alcohol and fatty food?

Let's think about how we react to suffering. For example, when a child falls and grazes his knee. Or when a man complains of severe sciatica linked to a hernia, causing him such pain that he is unable to move. Or when a woman hears of the death of a friend and her heart tightens and she feels she is suffocating and breaks out in terrible eczema. Or when a student fails an exam and her back and neck become tense and stiff. What goes on in our minds and bodies in these situations? It is precisely at moments like these that our mind steps in. It moves to shield us from hurt, trying, in any way it can, to stop the pain that is causing us suffering. The child goes to his mother, still crying, and she cleans the graze, puts on a plaster, then kisses him and convinces him that the pain has gone away. The man suffering from sciatica will see a doctor and be prescribed an anti-inflammatory. A psychiatrist or a psychotherapist will help the bereaved woman to feel better and will give her hydrocortisone for her eczema. The student will find a physiotherapist or an osteopath to treat her stiff neck.

What do these examples tell us? When we turn to medicine and therapy, this is the message we're sending to our bodies: 'You were wrong, you're not suffering.' And yet the fall, the back pain, the bereavement and the failed exam were all very real.

By helping us to escape from situations that cause us pain, our minds actually lead us away from where the solution might lie.

The Message of Illness

Could it be that we have lost the habit of trusting our bodies? Why don't we pay more attention to the messages they send us? We have been taught from birth that pain is a sign of weakness, and that it should not be allowed to express itself. We create a cognitive dissonance between our sensations and the way we perceive the problem. In other words, we have become deaf and blind to our bodies' alarm signals. It's as though we heard our phone ring but rejected the call before we even knew who was trying to contact us.

Let's try to decode this message. As we have seen, when we fall ill it's because our body has grown weak and vulnerable to the viruses, microbes and bacteria that are constantly attacking it. Why can it no longer defend itself? It is now well known that pollution caused by chemicals, emissions, pesticides and heavy metals takes its toll on our bodies by disrupting our hormones, which can affect the growth and behaviour of our cells. Can we, as individuals, limit our exposure to these pollutants? No (although we can all take steps to reduce our impact on the environment). And can we eliminate the viruses, microbes and bacteria that are all around us? No.

Given all this, what steps can we take to heal ourselves? This is where the teachings of traditional and alternative medicine come into play, placing the emotions at the centre of their healing practice:

- Chinese medicine dates back 2,500 years, and its effectiveness is now fully acknowledged, even in the West. It demonstrates the important role that painful emotions play in the emergence of illness. For example, great sadness affects the lungs, anger damages the liver, and fear harms the kidneys.

- Acupuncture is based on the flow of energy through the body via invisible meridians, and highlights the impact of unpleasant emotions on our vital organs.

- Emotional Freedom Technique (EFT) involves stimulating certain points on these meridians, while speaking out loud in a positive way about a difficult past experience.

- Hypnosis allows us to revisit a difficult emotion, reimagining it as a positive event that we appropriate for ourselves.

- Sophrology seeks to alter emotions by using breathing techniques and focusing on positive memories.

- Kinesiology tests muscular responses in order to identify the exact point where the body has developed an imbalance in response to an emotion caused by a traumatic event.

- Iridology is based on the idea that the health of the whole body can be examined by studying the iris. Every unpleasant emotion creates a visible mark in the eye.

- The flower remedies developed by Dr Bach help us to manage our feelings by working on our strongest emotions: hypersensitivity, dejection, fear, loneliness, despair and excessive anxiety.

- There is even a form of osteopathy that identifies harmful emotions and evacuates them by applying pressure on the trigger points.

- Finally, aromatherapy, shiatsu, somatotherapy, Eye Movement Desensitisation and Reprocessing (EMDR, a technique that treats the effects of traumatic experiences by associating them with specific eye movements) and other approaches all rely on seeking and managing disruptive emotions and trauma.

The body is a receptacle for our emotional difficulties. Through illness, our organism sends us the positive signal that we are capable of opening our eyes to these difficulties, and of freeing ourselves from them.

The Link Between Our Bodies and Our Emotions

All difficult emotions – even those experienced before birth – can have an impact on our bodies. Irritation, anger, abandonment, guilt, humiliation, shame, injustice, sadness, rejection, fear and betrayal: all emotional wounds create a 'knot' within our bodies that blocks the energy flowing through our cells. When we're young and healthy, most of us are strong enough to carry on despite this blockage, but pollution, fatigue, stress and the passing of time make the body less able to combat the problem.

As a result, when an unpleasant emotion reactivates our early emotional wounds, our weakened body succumbs to illness. Of course, we must rely on medication to reduce our pain and prevent pathogens proliferating, but if we want to eradicate the problem once and for all we need to be aware that our bodies are drawing our attention to an old wound that we have not healed – that we may not even be aware of. In other words, our body can no longer tackle this knot alone, and is asking for it to be removed.

During my workshops, participants often insist: 'The problem isn't emotional, I really am experiencing pain.' We shouldn't confuse cause and effect. A difficult emotion has triggered a malfunction in your cells, which has allowed the pathology to develop within you. The illness is there, and it's real. If you undergo medical examinations, they will reveal an inflammation, bacteria, a virus or a torn muscle. The body expresses its malaise through a very real illness. So why not turn to psychiatry, psychology or psychoanalysis for a solution? These therapies focus on our emotions, and we use them to help us conquer neuroses, get over depression, manage stress, improve our self-confidence, cure our phobias, and come to terms with our unhappy memories. It never occurs to us, however, to draw on them to treat physical pain (sciatica or a stiff neck, for example), and even less a cold or diarrhoea. They have the potential to help us, but we ignore them because we haven't learned to see the link between physical illness and our emotions. Nevertheless, this link with the emotions holds the key to a cure.

Let's think about illnesses that recur in successive generations. The internationally renowned psychologist and psychotherapist Anne Ancelin Schützenberger conducted many clinical studies, especially with cancer patients, over a period of twenty years. Her approach united conventional medicine and psychotherapy, and she discovered surprising instances of repetition over generations. One encounter, with a 35-year-old Swiss woman who believed herself doomed to die, proved crucial to Schützenberger's ideas. Above the woman's bed there was a portrait of her mother, who had died of cancer . . . at the age of thirty-five. Schützenberger suggested that the young woman might be unconsciously identifying herself with her mother, to the point of repeating her fate. This insight changed the patient's life, and the course of Schützenberger's research. By understanding it, we are not 'obliged' to carry our family's injuries, it is possible to stop the repetition. As she said, 'Becoming aware of repetitions is sometimes enough to strengthen a person's emotions to the point that they can free themselves from their unconscious family loyalties.'

Similarly, I remember meeting a woman of about forty whose vision was deteriorating very quickly. She feared going blind, as her mother and grandmother had done before her, but an eye examination revealed no abnormalities. The problem seemed to be genetic, and incurable. She then sought the help of Michelle Duhamel, a therapist specialising in the use of 'family constellations', a technique for managing transgenerational conflicts through group therapy. The woman also conducted extensive research into her own family tree – and everything became clear!

She was astonished to discover that 200 years earlier, one of her ancestors had, at the age of four, witnessed the massacre of her whole village by troops fighting for Napoleon III. Without a doubt, this traumatised little girl had wished with all her might 'never to see . . . that again'. Here was the key to healing the woman's illness. *Never seeing again*: that was the vital piece of emotional information she had inherited from her ancestors.

She then went through a process of 'cleansing' the emotional wounds of her family line, and her vision returned.

Modern medicine does acknowledge that emotions can lie at the heart of illness, and the field of psychoneuroimmunology is growing fast. Its basic principle is that stress can damage the immune system to the point that it becomes vulnerable to microbes, viruses and bacteria.

Every illness carries a message from our body, information linking the illness to an emotional wound. This is why exploring the difficult episodes of our lives will have a very real effect on our health. Similarly, identifying the origin of an illness can also present difficult episodes in the future.

Chapter 4

Escaping the Cycle of Illness

Listening to What Our Bodies Are Telling Us

D isease – a complex and multifactorial phenomenon – is frequently rooted in an unpleasant emotion. Whether this emotion was experienced recently or long ago, it has made its way deep inside us to create a knot in our energy flow. Over time, this knot causes us to experience health problems. The blockage in our energy makes us fragile and more vulnerable to microbes, viruses and other pathologies that are all around us, or even already within us. Whichever course of action we take, we must always remember the importance of consulting a doctor to treat the infection, the virus or the pain as soon as the first symptoms appear.

At the same time, it is vital to unravel this knot in our energy: releasing the blockage will prevent the illness returning. But how can this be done? We might be tempted to turn to a healer, a hypnotist or any specialist working with the body's energy. Therapists can often help if the pain is unbearable (for example, in cases of eczema or burns) but their actions alone are not enough. It is extremely important to ask yourself questions about the causes of your illness, to avoid the problem returning or expressing itself in the form of a different illness.

This course of action is unconventional, I agree, but it is vital, because as soon as our suffering is alleviated, the alarm signals are muted and we stop trying to understand what caused the pain. We think we are free of it, but this is a mistake, because the cause of the blockage in our energy flow remains, increasing the impact of the illness on our body. It is therefore essential to continue the search for its origin.

In the long term, you will need to consult a therapist but also play an active role in your own healing. Seek out the trigger of your illness in order to prevent it returning. You'll be surprised what you can achieve! If you still need convincing, here is Dr Albert Schweitzer's advice: 'All patients carry their own medicine inside them. They come to us not knowing this simple truth. We excel when we give the doctor within each patient the opportunity to get to work.'

If you are ill, here is a reason to be cheerful: your body is calling your attention to a difficult emotion, and you can expel it by becoming aware of it.

Identifying the Trigger Event

Identifying the destabilising emotion provides the key to your freedom. What sort of emotion might it be? An unkind remark, a disappointment, fear, a piece of bad news, bereavement, separation, redundancy, failure, feelings of guilt, betrayal, an argument, a sense of shame ... any challenging situation can open an old wound, one that we perhaps didn't even know existed.

Note down any disturbing events that occurred a few hours, days, weeks or months before you fell ill.

- Example: tonsillitis. Two days earlier: argument with such-and-such, impossible to express my feelings, I spent the evening brooding over what I should have said.

- _____
  _____
  _____

- _____
  _____
  _____

- _____
  _____
  _____

It's usually easy to remember a health problem that developed straight after a bereavement, but realising that we caught a cold, a bug or tonsillitis in the wake of an ordinary but unpleasant remark made by an acquaintance is much less straightforward. So why can these seemingly trivial occurrences cause as much harm as a traumatic event? Simply because they are the **aftershocks** of a series of emotional **earthquakes** experienced during childhood.

From now on, as soon as you begin to feel ill, try to remember any arguments or unpleasant experiences that have occurred recently. Note down these causes in a book dedicated to your health. Listening to your body and your emotions will make it easier to recognise the link between a symptom (the illness) and the trigger event (the difficult emotion experienced in the past that is being reactivated).

Initially, the pain we experience may be barely perceptible, so that when it eventually worsens, over the course of a few weeks, we can no longer remember what set it off. Similarly,

THE KEY TO YOUR ENERGY

an illness may result from a whole series of events, as in the case of a girl I knew who was in perfect health. One night she decided to spend the evening at a nightclub with her friends. During the evening, the boy she was secretly in love with left with her best friend: first emotional shock. Over the following days, she gave in to the friend who had often tried to persuade her to smoke marijuana. She did it to forget her sadness, but in the end the lethargy it induced made her neglect her studies. Three months later, her parents saw her terrible exam results and reacted harshly, knowing nothing of what had gone on: 'You've got no idea of the sacrifices we made to send you to university. You're selfish and irresponsible.' The young student felt guilty: second emotional shock. Then, not understanding why she had become such an 'underachiever', she fell into depression: third emotional shock. By this stage, she was really ill. Since that evening in the nightclub, so much time had passed that it was difficult to trace her problems back to it. Uncovering the original emotion isn't always straightforward, but luckily there are solutions.

Identifying the Emotional Cause

When we manage to make sense of the emotional cause of an illness, the healing process moves more quickly. You'll see! If you haven't identified your emotional wound yet, ask yourself the following questions. They will help you identify one of the potential sources of your illness. In this exercise, don't hold back: try not to feel self-conscious, and note down anything that springs to mind as honestly as you can.

TECHNIQUE 2

Identifying the trigger event

1. Consult a doctor, then ask yourself if you have ever experienced this type of illness before.

2. If you have, think back to when it occurred. Whom had you met shortly before? Did somebody say something that annoyed you?

3. Does this past incident have any connection to what is happening now?

4. Close your eyes and think about your illness. What emotion springs to mind? Fear, betrayal, sadness, humiliation, hatred, rejection, injustice, guilt, anger, powerlessness, abandonment, frustration . . . ? Note it down, because this is the painful emotion that needs to be healed.

5. Is this illness benefitting you in some way? (Being ill is sometimes a way of having someone else look after you. Or does this illness mean you can avoid thinking about a situation that's worrying you? Is it giving you time to rest, something you don't usually allow yourself? Is it an escape from work? Or is it letting you spend time with someone you love? Are you avoiding responsibility, or a situation that makes you feel trapped? Is it a way of postponing a decision, or attracting somebody's attention?)

6. Do you feel guilty? (Do you want to tell somebody to stop doing something, or find a way out of a particular situation?)

Chapter 5

The Emotional Symbolism of Illness

No therapy can claim to provide the only possible cure, simply because we are complex beings and diseases have all manner of different causes. The following suggestions therefore constitute one among many possible approaches to tackling illness, the most obvious being the approach of conventional medicine. Let's return to the idea of identifying the painful emotion that may be to blame for our illness. If you are finding it difficult to pinpoint this emotion, you may find clues by referring to the symbolism of illness. There are some helpful books giving interpretations of common symptoms: *The Complete Dictionary of Ailments and Diseases* by Jacques Martel and *What Your Aches and Pains Are Telling You* by Michel Odoul. These are just two examples of therapists who have carried out detailed observational work to establish connections between different ailments and their corresponding emotions. The suggestions outlined here are based on data – just as we can interpret dreams, we can also interpret illnesses – but it is still necessary to consult a doctor before trying any other approach: this is not like the method of 'biological decoding', which occasionally recommends stopping all conventional treatments.

The symbolic links outlined here arise from my observations of people I know and people who have attended my workshops.

These links are not stated as incontrovertible facts, because they are empirical observations of data and individuals, and cannot be presented as absolute truths. It would, in any case, be impossible to link every illness to one single emotional scenario. What follows is by no means a definitive system of diagnosis, rather a set of signposts to direct your own reflection. The real meaning is the one that speaks to you. It is possible to open your eyes to your trauma, but it is also possible to remain blind for your whole life. That is why this analysis of symbols can help us, by lifting a veil that has fallen over what we refuse to see.

- An **accident**, injury (resulting in haematoma, for example), or a **fracture** (even a small one such as a toe bone) could be the manifestation of a fear of a major change in the future. In the upper body (**arm, shoulder, collarbone, elbow**) the link may be to work. In the lower body (**leg, foot, hip, ankle**) it could be a more general concern (family, future, home). It could also represent some kind of self-reproach or guilt, or the inability to stop doing something even though we know it is harming us. This could take the form of overwork, addiction, or spending too much time on one activity such as video games.

- An **allergy** may manifest itself when we are confronted with a decision or a state of affairs that we cannot accept. It can flare up when we find ourselves in a situation that resembles a difficult scenario in our past.

- **Anorexia** may express a deep urge to seek security by controlling what we eat in order to get over severe disappointment linked to love or to life in general. This illness can occur after a bereavement or divorce, or when a figure of authority has let us down.

- Any problems affecting the **arms** or **hands** may be related to taking action, the fear of taking action, or to our career, and they often occur when we feel imprisoned in a new situation because of another person. The **elbow** seems to be related to fearing the consequences of an action that we have taken either by choice or because we have been forced to. Acute **shoulder** pain or capsulitis (frozen shoulder) could be due to resentment or dislike that we can't express, either because we're afraid of the person in question or because we think we're overreacting, or because the person is deceased, too old, or too far away. A **fractured wrist** may be linked to a desire to stop doing something that we've been forced to do, or that we have forced ourselves to do.

- **Back** problems may reveal a desire for protection or support, or show that we are trying to carry a heavy burden (professional, financial or domestic) without receiving any acknowledgement. It may also be a sign of wanting to help others before ourselves, fear of displeasing others, or guilt. It may also result from a blow that we haven't seen coming (that has crept up 'behind our back'). **Curvature of the spine** may be linked to feeling trapped between two impossible alternatives (between a father and a mother during a divorce, for example) or the feeling of being a nonentity in the face of some powerful authority.

- Painful wrists due to **carpal tunnel syndrome** may mean that we want to stop obeying certain orders because they go against our needs. We might be finding it difficult to question another person's choices: is this really what we want to be doing?

- A **cataract** may occur when a situation has caused us immense sadness, but we refuse to acknowledge that sadness and conceal it behind intense anger.

- A **cold** may arise as a result of a situation (domestic, romantic or professional) that we don't understand and that keeps us in a state of confusion.

- **Constipation** could be linked to a desire to maintain total control over our professional or family life due to fear, and a refusal to delegate or take time off. It may also occur when we hold back too much in our conversations and interactions with others.

- **Cystitis** can occur when our needs are not respected, or when we feel that the questions or attitudes of a family member or colleague are invasive.

- **Degenerative illnesses** such as Alzheimer's disease are accentuated by the accumulation of certain chemicals or heavy metals in the brain, and we may be more likely to suffer from them if we are feeling oppressed by a secret that we can't divulge, if we are repressing feelings of guilt (for something that we have done or that someone else has done and we have felt powerless to resist), or a difficult situation to which we cannot find a solution.

- **Diabetes** may be due to sadness caused by being constantly undervalued (including by ourselves) and a lack of recognition from those we love (sometimes because they have passed away).

- **Diarrhoea** can occur when we feel tied to a situation (romantic, domestic or professional) in which we feel uncomfortable, or when events or anxieties in our daily lives create too much stress.

- An **ear infection** may be linked to a desire not to hear things that make us sad or angry, such as arguments, criticism or reproaches.

- **Fever** may be caused by anger towards another person or ourselves, following an argument.

- **Herpes** may be caused by frustration or a feeling of being misunderstood.

- An **ingrowing nail** could indicate feelings of guilt or fear after having made a bad decision concerning our future.

- **Knee** problems may stem from resenting the advice of friends who try to explain *what is best for us*, and the impossibility of *bending* in the face of other people's opinions because we refuse to admit when they are right. This may be because, in the past, we have been too quick to accept instructions from others.

- Problems in the **legs, hips** or **sciatic nerve** may be linked to uncertainty or anxiety about the future caused by a new, stressful situation (an important meeting, moving house, the death of a loved one, retirement, redundancy, a break-up, etc.). They may also be caused by a drastic change of direction, risky financial or sentimental decisions, or more generally a fear of moving forward and facing the future.

- **Losing our voice** might be an expression of anger, fear or sadness that has not been expressed.

- Serious illnesses affecting the **lungs (bronchitis, pneumonia)** could be a sign of discouragement, sadness linked to feelings of guilt (and fear of burdening others), fear of not being able to get past an obstacle, or difficulty finding peace following an event that has called into question our place within the family or within society. They may also affect a child who feels themself to be a burden.

- **Migraines** seem to be linked to the feeling of reliving a past threat, and feeling unsafe. **Headaches** may be expressions of insecurity, difficulty in discussing a trauma, fear, anxiety, or tension caused by living in a state of oppression or submission to another person. They may also occur when we feel out of place.

- **Obesity** may be a way of creating a kind of *armour* to fend off repeated attacks or humiliations, or to protect ourselves from others or from their unwanted desires. It may also be a way of shielding ourselves from other things: the shame of feeling weak, failure to find our place (within the family when we were children, for example), a sense of worthlessness, being unable to change a difficult situation, or a fear of abandonment.

- **Osteoarthritis, rheumatism** and **inflamed joints** may be linked to low self-esteem, a sense of *worthlessness*, of always acting for others (through fear of displeasing them) rather than for one's own satisfaction, or to feeling guilty about getting angry when others don't guess how we're feeling . . . without us having to tell them.

- **Phlebitis** could be the manifestation of a build-up of annoyances and disappointments, or the result of denying ourselves happiness rather than risk further disappointment.

- Illnesses affecting the **prostate** may be linked to negative thoughts or feelings of guilt in relation to women/men, or to one woman/man in particular, or to feeling that our authority or value as a man has been called into question.

- **Psoriasis** may correspond to a double wound of abandonment (for example, a divorce followed by the death of a loved one, or a loss of mobility followed by redundancy).

- **Self-harm** can arise when we feel worthless compared to our peers, or unable to achieve what others expect of us.

- Any kind of **skin problem (eczema, erythema, itching)** may be connected to the wound of abandonment or loneliness, feeling oneself to be the victim in a scenario of separation (the loss of an important figure during childhood, divorce, the loss of a loved one, the arrival of a younger sibling), the rejection of a situation that angers us, whether or not we ourselves created it, or frustration at not being able to help someone.

- A **slipped disc** could be due to feeling obliged to support our entire family or business, and not feeling any gratification or benefit. We may feel *crushed* by debt, family burdens, or a job that we no longer find fulfilling.

- A **stroke** may occur after an emotional trauma linked to the loss of (or the fear of losing) something very important to us: losing custody of a child, a business failure, being made redundant, the prospect of retirement, an unexpected break-up, being thrown out of our home, the sudden death of a loved one, etc.

- Problems with our **teeth** may correspond to a loss of self-confidence, a fear of acting on a decision we have made, or a sense of being unable to fulfil a task we have set ourselves. Toothache may be linked to anger at a feeling of having been deceived.

- **Thyroid** problems could be connected to difficulty expressing ourselves, a feeling of not being listened to, or the fear of allowing ourselves to 'be ourselves' in the presence of others; everything that can be related to your place in life.

- **Tinnitus** could be linked to the fear of saying too much, the sense that our words have misrepresented our thoughts, the fear that someone may behave violently towards us if we express our feelings or the result of putting too much pressure on ourselves.

From now on, if you have a cold, lose your voice, or are suffering from an inflamed elbow, don't say: 'I've caught a cold . . .' 'I talked too much . . .' 'I carried something too heavy . . .' Get into the habit of asking yourself the following questions: 'The day before, or the week before, who did I see? What did I do? What happened to annoy me? Which emotional wound came to the fore?' If there isn't an obvious cause and effect, make use of the list of the symbolism of illnesses and open your eyes to what your body is trying to tell you. Sometimes, disruptions in our energy flow are expressed in the form of illnesses, but they are also revealed during difficult moments in our lives. It is also common for difficult moments and illnesses to occur simultaneously.

Changes in our symptoms over time can be especially good indicators of our emotional state. For example, Lucas, a young neighbour of mine whose parents are divorced, lives mainly with his mother. When Lucas used to visit his father, he was mistreated, because that was the only way his father had found to hurt his ex-wife. When Lucas returned to his mother, he was often suffering from **gastroenteritis**, a clear manifestation of a feeling of guilt and anger against himself for not having managed to stand up to his father. As he grew older, Lucas became increasingly able to oppose his father, who now behaves less harshly towards him but often humiliates him with comments that are meant to be 'funny'. Now, when Lucas leaves his father's house, he catches a **cold**, a sign of great confusion: he can't understand his father's behaviour.

Another example illustrates the link between our emotions and our illnesses perfectly. Michel is a 65-year-old art teacher who lives with his wife in Paris, while their daughters live in the South of France. Over the winter, his wife fell ill with severe **bronchitis** for the first time in her life. The long separation from their daughters had affected her state of mind. The daughters insisted that their parents should move to live closer to them, 'away from all the pollution', but for Michel abandoning his students seemed inconceivable. He began to suffer from **knee** pain. The symbolism of this symptom indicates that Michel probably didn't want to give in to his daughters' arguments. He consulted a doctor, who arranged for him to have surgery in the autumn. After visiting his daughters several times, Michel changed his mind about moving, and after that his **hip** was painful instead. Pain in this area can indicate fear of an unknown situation. Michel's doctor saw him in October, prior to the scheduled operation, but now the X-rays showed that the problem had indeed shifted to his hip. Keeping an eye on each of our physical problems, and treating them as alarm bells alerting us to emotional difficulties, can help us avoid all sorts of difficult and unnecessary situations.

Unless we commit to studying our emotions and our relationships with others, our body will continue to express our unhappiness through gradually evolving illnesses. Opening our eyes to the relationships between emotions and symptoms is the first step towards healing.

Chapter 6

You Have the Power to Turn Things Around

Would you like to rediscover your inner strength? It's time to reconnect with something you'd forgotten all about: that invisible energy that has the power to stimulate your immune system. You're going to reclaim something that has been neglected for too long: the infinite power that exists inside you.

The Solution Is Within

Until now, your automatic reaction has been to 'get rid' of your health worries by consulting a specialist. When I developed my double slipped discs, I did the same. I saw a doctor, who conducted an MRI scan and diagnosed a spinal problem. He prescribed a muscle relaxant and powerful anti-inflammatories, alongside other medication to treat the side effects of the two first ones. The back pain improved slightly. I could sleep at night now, but during the day I was still in great pain, and couldn't drive or work because it was so painful to sit down. If the pain had stopped completely at that point, I certainly wouldn't have investigated any further, and perhaps I would have developed another slipped disc the following year.

I was now in less pain, thanks to the medication, and I was fully aware that my condition was the manifestation of an old emotion that was preventing the circulation of energy through my body. I decided to turn to an acupuncturist to unravel the knots in my energy. He inserted needles into the painful areas, and the pain receded a little further. Two weeks later I consulted a hypnotist, and this helped a lot. The pain was now bearable, so I stopped taking my medication, as my doctor had recommended.

Some symptoms lingered (luckily for me, as it turned out), so I decided to investigate the emotional origin of this **back pain**. Determined to put an end to it once and for all, I consulted a therapist to help me explore the reasons for this problem. I followed up this investigation with a few sessions of EFT (Emotional Freedom Technique), a psychological and physical practice that deprogrammes certain emotions by stimulating the energy meridians described in Chinese medicine, while reciting liberating phrases linked to our wounds. By the end of my fourth session, the pain had stopped. In the end, I dealt with the **double slipped discs** in two months without needing an operation. It was wonderful to get up in the morning and feel my back completely free of stiffness and pain, but it was even more exciting to know that I had really *listened* to my body *expressing itself* for the first time.

What did I learn from this experience? The answer lay in managing the energy present in my body, and the words I recited during the EFT sessions. My Cartesian mind needed to work out exactly what this energy was, and why phrases linked to my wound had been so effective in removing the last traces of pain.

It was only when I conducted interviews with several physicists that everything began to make sense. They explained that our bodies are made up of billions of molecules, each of which is composed of several atoms. An atom is 0.0001 per cent matter (the neutron and the electrons) and 99.9999 per cent empty space, but according to quantum physics this empty space is actually filled with **energy** and **information.**

This was a revelation! Our body contains almost a hundred times more energy and information than matter (if we stick to the first two decimal places, but if we take all the numbers after the point, it's more like a million times more). Therefore, limiting ourselves to only treating the tangible and visible part of our organism (the 0.0001 per cent matter) and neglecting to consider the energy and emotional information that make up the 99.9999 per cent is, mathematically speaking, a mistake.

*Once illness has set in, you should turn to conventional medicine to ensure that it doesn't get worse. Then, in order to make a long-term difference, use the prescribed medication alongside therapy or practices that use spoken rituals (rich in **information**) and draw on the strength of your own conviction (phrases recited with **energy**). Don't forget: this information and this energy make up 99 per cent of our bodies, and can therefore be extremely effective.*

The Link Between Body and Energy

This relationship between the body and its energy was made even clearer to me by the doctor and acupuncturist Robert Corvisier, when discussing a situation that we have all encountered at some point:* when faced with a stressful situation, it is very common to suffer from diarrhoea. Why is this almost

* *Soigner avec l'acupuncture* (Éditions Dunod, 2017)

inevitable? Corvisier, an expert in Chinese medicine, explains that stress creates heat in the body and, in reaction to this sudden rise in energy, the body tries to re-establish its temperature balance by evacuating the excess heat via the digestive tract, resulting in diarrhoea. This unpleasant reaction, which we instinctively want to prevent, is nonetheless the only way for our body to free itself of excess energy in moments of stress.

If we enquire further into the reasons for our stress, it may be linked to emotions such as sadness (which affects the lungs), anger (which affects the liver), anxiety or worry (which upset the stomach or the spleen), or fear (which creates imbalance in the kidneys). Given that the origin of the pain is different depending on the person's background, does it make sense to treat all cases of diarrhoea with the same medication? Medication is absolutely vital from a clinical perspective, in order to avoid the risk of dehydration (especially in children), but can it tackle the problem of stress, and stop it causing diarrhoea in the future? Might we be able to put an end to this process of self-regulation, and if so how could the excess energy be expelled?

Let's take an example from my own personal experience, and use it to explore this idea further. Over twenty years ago, I was hired by a production company to adapt TV game-show formats from abroad for French television, and the head of entertainment at the time was an absolute dragon. If viewing figures were good, it was thanks to her genius; if they were low, it was my fault. So I would have a bad case of the runs five or six times a week. At the time, I went to see a doctor in an attempt to manage the problem (I'd often need to go in the middle of a meeting, and I wasn't about to get a map of all the toilets in the building tattooed on the back of my hand). The problem persisted despite the anti-diarrhoea medication, but it disappeared *as if by magic* the day I quit my job. Stress and diarrhoea were most certainly connected.

When illness strikes, shift your focus! Forget about the parts of your body you can touch. We're mostly made up of something impalpable and invisible: energy and information. Our organism possesses a power that we are far from understanding. When we see things from this angle, we allow our bodies to heal themselves.

Chapter 7

Self-Healing

As I continued my investigations, I observed that sometimes our health improves as if by magic as soon as we make an appointment with a therapist, simply because we trust that they will cure us. How many of us have arrived at the dentist or the doctor's surgery and said, 'It was hurting before, but it's stopped now'? Or perhaps we feel better as soon as we leave the appointment, before we've even collected our medication: 'I was so worried it was something serious, but the doctor told me it wasn't, and now the pain has completely disappeared.' It's true: what could be more comforting than a doctor telling us we're healthy? We allow ourselves to feel better, and that's one proof of the extraordinary power of our minds, and of self-healing. But one question was still bothering me: our minds spend so much time trying to hide the truth from us, but could they also be our allies? Why do some people recover and others not? Does it all depend on our *state of mind*?

The Power of Our Minds

It wasn't until I looked back over three of my own experiences that a theory began to form in my mind. When I was seventeen, a wart began to develop on my hand. As a child I'd had an enormous one on my foot, and I still remembered the pain of having it removed. The last thing I wanted was to have this one taken off in the same way, but it kept on growing, and eventually, after a year, I knew I had to do something about it.

Strangely, every time I happened to look at the wart, the word *guilt* came into my mind. I thought about when it had first appeared, and realised that it was when I'd just broken up with my boyfriend in a rather clumsy way. A while later, I stared at the horrible wart and, letting my instinct guide me, I said: 'Listen, wart, I know you're there because I acted insensitively when I broke up with him. Yes, I do feel guilty for having left him so abruptly, but I was inexperienced and now I understand. I'm going to close my hand and not look at you for three days. When I look again, you'll have disappeared.' I then forced myself not to look at the palm of my hand for three days (I could have said two days or four days, it wouldn't have made any difference). I even managed to forget about it. Imagine my surprise when, after the three days, I discovered that the skin of my palm was completely clear. It seems unbelievable – and I admit it's hard to believe unless you've actually experienced it – but I've never forgotten my amazement at finding my skin restored to normal.

Two years later, I met a man who fulfilled all the criteria I had *unconsciously* set for my perfect partner. The problem was that we argued constantly. I didn't know it at the time, but this turned out to be a piece of luck. Every time we argued, I would begin a bout of **cystitis**. The cycle was obvious: a fierce argument followed by this **inflammation**. It was too clear to ignore: given that it was my getting angry that triggered the infection, it was nothing to do with microbes, and everything to do with my mind. The attacks of cystitis were a result of our arguments, so I could choose to react to our disagreements in a different way. I made a promise to myself out loud: 'From now on, I will never have cystitis again.' It's a common problem in my family, but I have now become the only one who never suffers from it.

My experience of perimenopause also changed the way I thought about these issues. My friends often complained of hot flushes, weight gain and irritability, and I was experiencing the same symptoms. I read several books about the symbolism of illnesses, and discovered that part of the problem was a tendency to accept certain symptoms as being inevitable. I simply needed to decide that these symptoms wouldn't affect me, but my mind had its doubts, telling me that it was a waste of time because I'd already been experiencing the problems for several months. Then I remembered my experience with cystitis and the wart, so I said to my body, in a loud, clear voice, with strength and conviction: 'You're strong enough to bounce back after difficult experiences, so you're strong enough not to embarrass me with hot flushes, weight gain and irritability.' After a few days, the symptoms melted away and never came back!

Talking to Your Body

As you will have noticed, it's important to talk to yourself, out loud. Does talking to your body feel awkward? Don't worry – you probably already do it unconsciously. Have you ever said things like, 'I'm sick of this aching back,' 'What am I going to do about my stiff joints?' 'I'm tired of my fat stomach,' 'I hate my hair,' 'I'm ugly,' 'I don't like my skin' or 'Damn this sore elbow'? You're already talking to your body without realising it.

It rarely occurs to us to say, 'Thank you, back, I've realised where the problem is,' but we need to learn to pay more attention to the messages we're sending our bodies. I once pointed out to a man suffering from recurrent diarrhoea that he often used the phrase 'I don't give a shit', and to a woman suffering from back pain that she frequently complained about her friends, saying she wanted them 'off her back'. Let's take more care with our words and how we use them in relation to our bodies.

Why does the way we communicate with our bodies have such an impact on our healing? What exactly is happening? I decided to look for a scientific explanation. Giacomo Rizzolatti was a doctor, biologist and professor of physiology in the Faculty of Medicine at Parma University, and in the 1990s he showed that our brains contain mirror neurons. These neurons allow babies to learn new actions through mimicry, but they also do something else, which is relevant to us here: these grey cells make our brain believe that a situation *that we imagine is real* is actually real. For example, if I drink a glass of water, certain areas of my brain are stimulated. If I pretend to drink a glass of water, and actually think I am doing so, then the same areas of the brain react. The same thing happens to another person's brain if they think I am drinking a glass of water. The results of this study were confirmed by other researchers in 2010, and they show that these mirror neurons affect our perception of reality: our brains do not differentiate between a real action and an imagined action that we believe to be real.

You can try a little experiment to demonstrate this: imagine you're rolling a small bit of aluminium foil between your fingers. Now put it in your mouth, between your back teeth, and bite down hard on it. You see? You immediately feel a little shiver of discomfort, as though the ball really were being ground between your teeth; but it's all in your imagination. Even more strangely, you may perhaps have felt this unpleasant sensation just by reading these last few lines. Such is the power of our mirror neurons.

Imagining that a situation is real makes it an authentic situation as far as your brain is concerned: the power of intention is extremely strong. Remember, your body is made up of

0.0001 *per cent matter, and* 99.9999 *per cent energy and information.* **The power of intention** *means ensuring that every little bit of energy in your atoms receives a clear message:* '*Here is how I am going to heal.*'

TECHNIQUE 3

Self-healing

1. Are you ill? Something important is happening: your body is sending you a message in the form of a symptom. It's up to you to work out what the symptom means.

2. Try to find the emotional event that triggered this illness. If you can't, ask yourself the questions from technique 2. If you still can't find the answer, or you want to look for further possibilities, consult the list of illnesses and their symbolism in Chapter 5.

3. Talk to your body. Say out loud that you want to get better, and thank it for its message: '**Thank you, body, I understand that this illness** [specify the illness] **is connected to the wound of** [specify the wound] **or to the experience of** [specify the painful event]. **You can stop the symptoms because I'm going to take steps to free myself.**' Talk to it like this every day, several times a day, but without getting angry, until the symptom disappears. There is no limit to how many times you can do it, and no situation in which it poses any danger to your health.

4. Last but not least: keep your promise. Work through techniques 5, 6, 7 and 8 and, if necessary, don't hesitate to ask a therapist to help you through this process of liberation.

These four steps worked brilliantly for a friend of mine who woke up one morning with bad **toothache**. He took painkillers, but the pain was still so bad it was making him nauseous. According to the symbolism of illnesses, toothache can mean that we don't feel equal to a task that we have set ourselves. At the time, my friend was preparing a photography exhibition, and had spent the previous two weeks going over his portfolio to make sure he didn't leave any out. I suggested that perhaps his body was expressing something he hadn't admitted to himself: was he afraid of not having enough material for his exhibition? Astounded, he admitted that this was true. I suggested that he should thank his body and reassure it. He was doubtful at first, but agreed to try, willing to do anything that might relieve the pain. He said, out loud and in a strong voice: 'Thank you, body, for having drawn my attention to this feeling, this fear of not having enough good photographs for my exhibition. I've understood, and you can take the pain away. Now I'm going to sort through all the best images, and I'll feel better.' After thanking his body, he promised to change his approach. Half an hour later, the pain had disappeared.

It's important to keep the promises you make to your body. It's your best friend, and if you listen to the messages it sends you and draw on the tools you need to change your own attitude, as well as using medication, you will get well for good.

The Key Is in the Intention

Every time you feel pain, talk to your body. In some cases, your own will (intention) will be strong enough to cure the problem immediately. That was the case for my bouts of cystitis. I followed my instinct and said very determinedly to my body: 'This only happens when we argue, so it's got nothing to do with microbes, and it won't ever happen again.'

Sometimes, it will take more time. It may be that the outcome depends on the emotional difficulty linked to the pathology.

TECHNIQUE 4

Strengthening the intention

You can easily strengthen your intention and therefore reduce your pain. This approach is inspired by shamanic practices.

1. Breathe in deeply through your nose and imagine that when you exhale, the breath leaves your body at the painful spot, as though the air were passing over the pain and expelling it.

2. Practise this exercise at least ten times in a row, focusing on visualisation and breathing. Feel free to carry on until the pain has disappeared. You'll see – it works!

3. There's another shamanic technique you can use: think about an animal you like – a lion, an elephant, a tiger, an eagle, a wolf, a squirrel . . . Now imagine this animal shrinking to the size of an atom. Pick it up and put it in your mouth. Allow your mind to transport it to the painful spot, then imagine what the animal might do to help you: it might lick the painful area to relieve inflammation, it might ease tense muscles, repair torn ligaments, or warm your throat. It is your ally, and will stay inside you as long as necessary. Don't forget to thank it.

For example, if sciatica flares up when you're planning a long car journey, talk to your body (with a phrase such as 'I know

I'm doing too much, and neglecting myself'), then take the time to breathe and *blow* the air past the painful area. Remember: this exercise isn't as easy as it sounds! Concentrating on your breathing for a stretch of time is no mean feat, because we have to stop thoughts about everything else in our lives distracting us.

Similarly, if you have a stomach ache, or a headache that doesn't ease off towards the evening, first try to identify the message your body is sending you, then perform the breathing exercise described above, and do it once more just before bed.

By harnessing of the power of intention, you will be helping the different parts of your body to reconnect with their growth mechanism. This mechanism is present in all of us before birth, and each of our cells has a memory of it. By allowing this vital energy to circulate once more, we are allowing our tissue to rebuild itself: self-healing can begin.

What is our intention? Do we genuinely want to get well? Or do other concerns take precedence? Do we put off tackling our health issues? Is our work more important? Do we prioritise looking after our family and children over ourselves? Is there some benefit for us in being ill? Are we prepared to work on our emotions or would we rather take the 'easy option' of handing over the task of healing to a therapist or to medication? Ask yourself these questions, answering as honestly as you can.

Chapter 8

Reassuring the Mind

From childhood, we learn to put our health in the hands of doctors and therapists. It is therefore likely that most of us have a little voice inside our heads saying that *talking to our bodies* isn't a realistic approach. How can we change our attitude and increase the power of our intention? We need to send a clear message to our Cartesian minds if we aren't to be held back by fear of failure. I've thought a lot about how to go about this, and it seems to me that the first step we take to ease our symptoms should be something 'normal', like taking medication, consulting a doctor, or seeing an acupuncturist or a homeopath. It's only after having accomplished this first step that we can really begin taking our emotional experience in hand by talking to our bodies.

Learning to React Differently

Medication can be useful not only for healing our bodies but also for alleviating our anxiety. This process can sometimes work even just with a placebo, which has no actual medicinal effect. Here is a very concrete example: one day, a patch of eczema began to develop on my arm, near my armpit. Apart from this small ailment I was in excellent health, and I couldn't identify the meaning behind this problem, even after asking myself all the questions set out in the previous chapters. According to the symbolism of illnesses, eczema can represent the pain of separation. This suggestion brought back some difficult memories, so I continued my investigation and looked into the problems associated with the armpit area, on the basis that the location of my eczema was sure to be significant. Sure enough, it was linked to a feeling of guilt at not having helped somebody enough.

I immediately burst into tears: I knew I'd found one of the potential causes of my illness. The pain wasn't severe, and the eczema was by no means unbearable. I thanked my body out loud for having drawn my attention to some difficult emotions I'd experienced in the past: a feeling of abandonment and a sense of guilt for not having realised that somebody was hoping for my help. It helped me a lot to realise that, at the time, I was unaware that the person in question was in trouble. I said out loud that I'd done what I could, and that I was sorry for letting my own suffering blind me to someone else's. Then I asked the person's forgiveness.

Aware that my mind might impede the healing process I had set in train (because at that time I was still wary of relying exclusively on the power of intention), I completed this technique by administering a neutral substance. I sprinkled talc over the patch of eczema, convinced that it would now disappear. I repeated these steps every day, morning and evening, and I still remember my sense of elation as the eczema gradually faded away until, about ten days later, it had completely gone!

Finally, I made sure to apologise to the person face-to-face: a very intense encounter that was the conclusive step in my complete recovery.

- *By remedying the symptom, you reassure your mind, and, by identifying the emotion, you tackle the cause. In this way, you address the problem from all angles and avoid your illness becoming chronic.*

- *If your disease is mild, with no severe pain or risk that bacteria, microbes or a virus may multiply, set your mind at rest by using a substance that will act as a placebo, making sure that (thanks to your mirror neurons) your mind believes that this substance really will help you to recover.*

My eczema disappeared quickly because I treated it as soon as it appeared. For a health problem that has existed for a number of years, the process may take longer and will be very dependent on the intention of each individual. The main thing is not to be discouraged!

Time to Heal

If we react as soon as symptoms appear, and if we immediately begin to seek their meaning, we increase our chances of a quick recovery. If we postpone this action, we lose the advantage of being able to link the illness with its painful emotion, and we increase the healing time, as this example shows.

A friend of mine had been suffering from an extremely painful ingrowing **toenail** for a year. Even antibiotics hadn't helped, and he was due to have an operation. The night before, I asked him if he wanted to identify the message his body was sending him. He was intrigued, and decided to try. I suggested it might be guilt at having made a bad decision, and he agreed, saying it was something to do with his family. After the operation, the pain disappeared, so he forgot to explore his emotional wound further. Two months later, the same problem began to develop on his other foot. I encouraged him to consult a doctor and take antibiotics in order to remove any worry that *it wouldn't work*, and then he spoke to his body, telling it that he had understood the hidden message (this fear transformed into guilt at having made a bad decision), that he couldn't reverse it now, that he had done his best and that he was counting on it to heal without an operation. The ingrowing nail righted itself within a few days.

When **serious illness** sets in, it means that many signs have already appeared, but we have refused to see them. We needn't worry, though, because there's still time to act and, even though healing might take a while, we mustn't give up too soon. We should remind ourselves that the initial emotional problem occurred days, weeks or even years ago, and our bodies have waited a long time before allowing illness to set in.

Why did my **eczema** appear at that exact moment? Why didn't it set in as soon as I felt the guilt at not having helped that person? My theory is that at the time, I wouldn't have understood the message, so my body chose to wait until I was in a position to take action.

THE FOUR KEYS TO HEALING

1. You've understood the message behind your illness, you've spoken to your body, you've thanked it for drawing your attention to an old problem that has now been reactivated. You've identified the original painful emotion, and have asked your body to expel the pain and the symptoms. Now explain to it (aloud) what your next steps will be (seeing a therapist, practising certain techniques), then visualise the cleansing of the painful area using the exhalation technique.

2. At the same time, you should see a doctor or therapist, and/or take medication in order to neutralise your mind and reassure yourself. Do something *that you usually do*, to give yourself every chance of success. If you are not

in severe pain and there is no risk of the illness spreading, use a placebo (a substance with no medicinal effect). This could be talc, water or simply a sticking plaster, as long as you are convinced it will help.

3. Reflect on the emotion your body has revealed, and on how you might tackle it in order to keep your promise. It may be linked to your lifestyle or your relationships with others. To explore this further, you could begin a course of therapy (EFT, EMDR, hypnosis, psychotherapy) to help you comprehend your emotional wound.

4. Repeat these steps **every day**, and give your body time to heal.

Armed with our awareness of this process, what should we do in the future if somebody causes us to experience an unpleasant emotion? Palpitations, anger, dislike, fear, shame: whatever the emotion, it is likely to have an impact on our body. Can we avoid this dysfunctional knot developing inside us? Of course. Seize the initiative, and talk to your body again: 'Thank you, body, for using these symptoms to show me that an old emotional problem is being reactivated. I'm aware that I've got a problem with this person or this situation, and that I need to understand the underlying wound. Please give me time to find its origin so that I can get rid of it, and don't make me go through another illness.' It's vital to keep your promise if you want to succeed.

Now you're ready to carry out a full repair of the cracks that life has opened up in you. Your energy will return and you'll feel better for it!

PART TWO

Activating Your Powers!

Chapter 9

Your Energy Reset

There are times in our lives when we feel as flat as a pancake. We have no strength. Our legs can't seem to carry us. We're helpless in the face of adversity, unable to make the right decision or take action. I used to think it was all just a matter of willpower, but the death of one of my best friends opened my eyes to other possibilities. I spent two years researching how certain factors – an accident, bereavement, trauma, parental neglect, aggressive remarks heard as a child – can weaken us so much that we experience chronic fatigue or a feeling of no longer being in control of our lives. What are the processes at work?

Rediscover Your Energy

I needed to understand the reason for this *inability to act*, so I began by reading psychiatry and psychology manuals, but also by consulting energy therapists. I realised that conventional medicine and alternative medicine come to the same conclusions, only using different terminology. It was astonishing how much they had in common. For example, I learned that when we are seriously injured our bodies protect us by producing endorphins, hormones that reduce our pain levels and thus prevent us going into cardiac arrest. When we are facing a difficult situation (moving house during childhood, the arrival of a younger brother or sister, the loss of a pet, a serious argument, threats, an unwelcome discovery, the absence of a parent experienced as abandonment, repeated humiliations, rape), our body reacts in the same way, by protecting us. How does it do this? When the suffering becomes unendurable, part of our mind escapes, to avoid us sinking into mental illness. We are **petrified** (impossible to react), followed by a **dissociation** (the feeling of no longer inhabiting our own body and observing as though we were outside the situation). This psychological process explains *memory loss* and the phenomenon of denial observed in those who have suffered severe trauma. Psychiatrists call this '**mental flight**', whereas energy therapists use the term '**soul loss**': different terms carrying the same symbolism. *Soul* is a key word here. Leaving aside its religious connotations, let's define the soul as the basis of our way of thinking, our self-belief and, above all, the point where our energies converge. When we undergo trauma, we are suddenly deprived of all that. We lose confidence in life, feel *empty inside*, and lose part of our energy as a result of the shock.

Given that our bodies are made up of a hundred times more energy and information than matter, it is easy to see how part of this energy could be affected by such a damaging experience. A crack opens up inside us, and our vital energy seeps out. Following the trauma, our bodies try to react by seeking to reconnect with the missing part, so you shouldn't be surprised if you sometimes feel exhausted and unable to move forward in your life in the way you want to. The good news is that there are ways of closing up the wound and regaining the lost energy.

What did you feel when you read those lines? Did you feel suddenly upset? Did tears come to your eyes? Did you realise that you are completely at a loss to understand a particular person's behaviour towards you? If so it is likely that, at some point in your life, part of your soul detached itself in order to protect you from unbearable emotional pain, and your whole being is now longing to be reunited. The following techniques go well beyond a simple process of reconstruction: they show how we can regain control of the energies within us.

Soul Recovery

Loan Miège, a medium and healer who has a degree in animal biology, has developed a very effective series of steps to regain this energy through a process of *soul recovery*, and I am very grateful to her.* I used her work as the basis for what follows, modifying it so that it can be used in any context.

The point where our energies converge naturally sits in the middle of the chest, where the solar plexus is located. However, when we experience emotional shock, some of our energy leaves the body and stays above the head, often on the left-hand side. This displaced energy is what we are aiming to reintegrate into our body.

You can memorise the steps involved, record them on your smartphone (leaving pauses to repeat the phrases) or you can read them with the book beside you. **Only those who are over eighteen,** and who are self-motivated, mature and capable of making their own decisions, can carry out this process of soul recovery, and they must only do so voluntarily. This process opens up our consciousness and, if you force a child (or adult) to undertake it 'for their own good', you could harm them. You would be imposing your own will on them, thus taking away some of their energy rather than restoring it. There is one exception: for a child over sixteen with a severe health problem; but always on condition that he/she is mature and entering into the process voluntarily. Still, if the child says 'no' or 'not now', they aren't ready. Don't worry: you can try to help them (whatever their age) by repairing **yourself** first.

* Her book is *À la rencontre des Esprits de la Nature* (Éditions Exergue, 2014).

We have all been through ordeals in our lives, and I therefore recommend that everybody attempt this process of soul recovery. Some later steps may not work if this has not been completed. Please read the entire chapter for this important recommendation.

TECHNIQUE 5

Soul recovery following a shock

1. Create a sacred space: find somewhere peaceful, and light incense or a candle. Sit on the floor or on a chair. Remind yourself that you are about to have an important experience.

2. Call on two higher beings from this list: God, Jesus, Mary, Yahweh, Allah, Buddha, Ganesh, one of the archangels (Gabriel, Michael, Raphael, Uriel, etc.), the universe, 'beings of light' or your guardian angel. You will need two, and they need to be immensely powerful in order to overcome potential resistance. For this reason, don't choose family members who have passed away, even if they are your guides. These two 'beings of light' (as we may call them) take up their positions at your side. They are your witnesses and ensure that the steps will proceed as they should. Relax. Relax your back, your neck and your shoulders, and take a deep breath in through your mouth, three times.

3. With your eyes open or closed, visualise the presence of these two beings of light, as their love and goodwill

surround you. If you can't visualise them, carry on: the process will still work.

4. Say out loud: '**Please**, [names of your chosen higher 'beings of light'], **purify all the parts of my soul, within me and outside me.**'

5. Take a deep breath in, then say out loud, confidently, '**My soul, if there was a time when you were suffering, and you needed to distance yourself from me, please know that I am now able to hold you inside me.**' Raise your arms straight above your head, then lean to the left or to the right, it doesn't matter, and try to come into contact with your missing energies (you will feel a warmth, a prickling, or some resistance). Then say: '**Please**, [names of your chosen 'beings of light'], **place all the missing parts of my soul in my hands.**' Then straighten up so that your arms are once again directly over your head.

6. Now say: '**I invite all the parts of my soul to take their place in the centre of my chest.**' As you say these words, bring your hands and your energy back down through the top of your head, then your neck, and further down, until your hands are crossed over your chest. Now add: '**My soul, take up your place again, in confidence and love.**' Thank your chosen beings of light. This is an important moment, because you have just taken a very significant step. It is normal to feel strong emotions (sadness, joy or peace) or physical sensations (contraction, heaviness or fatigue).

Continue with the soul recovery following an energy theft (technique 6) or, if you are tired, stop there and rest, and don't carry out any more soul recovery exercises for at least two weeks.

As we can see from these instructions, it isn't necessary to remember every difficult event in our lives, because we simply evoke 'the time when you were suffering'.

The psychotherapist Jacques Roques pointed out to me that a variation of these steps is used in psychotherapy and is known as the 'light stream' technique.* This practice involves visualising infinite energy coming from the cosmos. The is energy is warm and benevolent, and enters through the top of the head, spreading through the body all the way to the feet before flowing out into the earth, which absorbs it.

An example of this technique in action is that of François-Olivier Stephan, a doctor, osteopath and homeopath whom I met at a conference. He told me he'd read *Les Blessures du silence* (*The Wounds of Silence*), a novel in which I evoke this technique. 'When I read about this technique, I realised that I was missing part of my energy. I was sure of it,' he explained. Then he went on: 'I learned the ritual by heart and began to carry it out, but I stopped. It was too strange. I went to bed, thinking I might try another day . . . Then, at one o'clock in the morning, I woke up and couldn't get back to sleep. I did the steps again, fully aware of what I was doing. I had a physical sensation of energy entering my body. Something like a joy being returned to its place. This soul recovery taught me that I had been missing something, because since doing it, my chronic fatigue has disappeared.'

I received equally moving testimony from Anne: 'After attending your workshops, I put the soul recovery into practice . . . and I haven't had a stomach ache for four days. I'm so happy! Ten

* Jacques Roques, *EMDR: une révolution thérapeutique* (Éditions Desclée de Brouwer, 2016) [2nd edition]

years of pain and now I'm cured! I feel as though I've put my past and its sufferings behind me.' As Dr Edward Bach wrote, 'To be in good health, we need to be in harmony with our soul.'

A loss of energy can express itself in the form of exhaustion or illness, but it can also take the form of psychological control. Despite our best efforts, we may be subjected to harassment that we can't possibly avoid. We may be paralysed in the presence of an abusive mother or a violent father, or be subjected to the sexual perversion of somebody we know. This state, which we might be tempted to describe as a *depression*, in the sense that it creates a void inside us, isn't caused by a lack of strength or an error in our behaviour. It is simply the result of certain things that happen to us, and certain encounters. If our friends see our reaction as a sign of weakness, insisting that 'You just have to tell them to stop,' or if they think we're exaggerating, or simply 'prone to that kind of thing', they're wrong. And it's a good thing they're wrong, because in fact we can always take action and find a way out, using another technique. Let's find out how.

Addiction and Affective Dependence = Loss of Energy

In the case of those who have suffered harassment, manipulation or sexual abuse, the part of their soul that has detached itself is not to be found just outside their bodies, above their heads. Instead, it has been taken by the abuser. This is theft! Energy therapists tell us that our *abuser* feeds off our weakness and our lost energy. Psychiatrists describe this as 'unconscious vampirism', and it creates a hold over the victim. The 'vampire' can be a parent, spouse, friend or colleague and, if the (physical or mental) violence is repeated, there's a chance that the victim may lose so much energy that they may unconsciously try to compensate through addiction (to food, alcohol, drugs, etc.). This theory of theft provides an interesting explanation of why victims may feel trapped in a situation – a feeling that they themselves find hard to understand. Why can't we escape, even though we're being abused? Because the abuser has taken part of our energy. Why do we return to a love that we know is harmful? Again, because the abuser has our energy: it isn't the persecutor we're attached to, i t's our own piece of light. We can't abandon a part of ourselves. Many people have asked me why they can't stop thinking about someone fifteen years after they last saw them. It isn't love or emotional dependence, rather that we're tied to the other person because they possess a part of us. This loss of soul can also affect those mistreated by their parents: they can't cut themselves off from the part of their soul that has been seized by their father or mother. Energy theft occurs when somebody has a hold over us. Fortunately, we can recover our energy and free ourselves from this unhealthy domination.

It is often thought that a victim can escape from a situation of domination or harassment simply by becoming more aware of their predicament and taking steps to improve their self-esteem. This is not true in most cases because of the 'brainwashing' that has taken place. This often takes the form of contradictory statements: the abuser can have a deeply destabilising effect on their victim by disguising criticisms as compliments ('That's a pretty dress – shame you're flat-chested') or by issuing conflicting instructions ('Get moving, you're so lazy!' and then, 'Why don't you have a rest? You should see how awful you look!'). For hundreds of victims I've encountered, the dominance began to break down as soon as they understood that their abuser had stolen a part of their energy.

Scholar Harassment

After publishing *Les Blessures du silence*, I was invited to speak at several conferences. At one of these, a man described not understanding why his nine-year-old son was being bullied at school. He'd been told that it was likely that his son was being manipulated by somebody he knew. The man couldn't think who this might be, so I asked him if his son had experienced a trauma that might have caused him to lose a part of his soul. The father then told me that he and his wife had been involved in a very serious accident some years previously. Their son, who was six when this had happened, had thought they were dead so he left a part of his energy, and it turned out that the bullying had begun around that time.

The psychologist and psychotherapist Patricia Serin uses a metaphor to describe this situation. We can imagine that we are a tree, and that a difficult experience creates a wound in our bark. The resulting hole is identified by bullies and abusers as a gap through which they can enter in order to gain a hold over us. They are not simply in love with us, they are attracted by the wound through which our vital energy escapes. This explains why, when we have been manipulated in one relationship, we may get involved with a similar kind of person in the future. We shouldn't feel guilty: we're not stupid or masochistic, it's simply a matter of energy. Victims are often kind, intelligent people who have good relationships with others. As we grow weaker, the abusers feed off our loss of energy in order to fill their own void, for they have also been victims of some kind of trauma.

If we are experiencing harassment, or have done in the past, it almost certainly means that we have lost a part of our energy due to a difficult experience, exploitation, mistreatment, incessant criticism (resulting in depression or anger), or manipulation by an acquaintance or family member. This has opened up a crack inside us that can easily be spotted by other potential abusers. In this case, it is vital to practise techniques 5 and then 6, focusing on the people involved. These techniques are aimed solely at adults, because only they are in a position to decide whether the moment is right for them. For children, it is better to see a psychotherapist and work on their emotions. If this therapist is also trained in EFT or EMDR, so much the better.

Remember, technique 6 can be used in relation to people who have died as well as those who are still alive. If you feel hesitant about doing it alone, you can ask someone you trust to recite the various phrases, which you will then repeat. You could also ask a therapist who is open to these methods for help: 'I would like to undertake these techniques, could you help me put them into practice?' Many doctors, psychotherapists and hypnotherapists have told me how effective these techniques have proved with their patients.

How do these techniques work? The idea is to enact a kind of 'exchange' whereby the missing part of our soul is returned to us. In other words, the other person gives back what they have stolen from us, and we help them to regain what somebody else took from them. This allows us to escape the cycle of destructive power struggles. If your resentment of your abuser makes you feel uncomfortable about helping them, remember that you're not doing it for their benefit, but because it's the **only way** they will ever return what belongs to you.

TECHNIQUE 6

Soul recovery following an energy theft

This step should be carried out alone (without making contact with the other person), and focuses on one person at a time. It's important to stop when you begin to feel tired. When you have completed two or three soul recoveries, wait at least two weeks before trying another one, otherwise your body will not have time to assimilate the recovered energy.

NEVER carry out soul recovery with your children.

If your child's behaviour towards you is problematic, it's because their own energy has been stolen as a result of parental conflict, divorce, or difficulties at home, at school or in their love life. Your child may take your energy in order to compensate for the loss of their own. This isn't a voluntary theft, and they are a victim first and foremost. In order for you both to regain your energy (and for the problematic behaviour to stop), carry out a soul recovery following an energy theft with each person who has destabilised you (except your children), one by one. The more you do, the more it will help. The only technique you can practise with your child is number 7, which restores peace.

1. Place two chairs opposite each other and sit down in one of them. Take a moment to acknowledge the importance of what you are about to do. The process needs the power of your intention in order to work.

2. Create a sacred space, relax, and call on two higher beings from this list: God, Jesus, Mary, Yahweh, Allah, Buddha, Ganesh, one of the archangels (Gabriel, Michael, Raphael, Uriel, etc.), the universe, 'beings of light' or your guardian angel. You will need two, and they need to be immensely powerful in order to overcome potential resistance. For this reason, don't choose family members who have passed away, even if they are your guides. These two 'beings of light' (as we may call them) take up their positions at your side. They

are your witnesses and ensure that the steps will proceed as they should. With your eyes open or closed, visualise the presence of these two beings of light, as their love and goodwill surround you. If you can't visualise them, carry on: the process will still work.

3. Say out loud: '**I thank** [your chosen higher 'beings of light'] **for helping me in this soul recovery with** [the name of the person who has repeatedly destabilised you] **in the form of an exchange.**'

4. Demonstrate your authority and say: '**Please,** [your chosen higher 'beings of light'], **order** [such-and-such] **to sit opposite me.**'

5. Now, tell the person who is on your mind what burdens you. Once something is said, it will no longer weigh on you, so allow yourself this relief. '**When you did . . . it was very hard . . .**'

6. Next, take a deep breath in and say out loud, confidently: '**Please,** [your chosen higher 'beings of light'], **order** [such-and-such] **to give back all the energy he/she has taken from me** [involuntarily] **in this life and in all the others.**'

7. Open your arms wide. Try to imagine a large ball of light appearing between you, and take hold of it. Try to sense a feeling, perhaps a prickling or a resistance between your open hands (the distance between your hands depends on the quantity of energy that you are going to regain). If you can't sense this, it will be happening anyway.

8. Keep your hands open and your arms outstretched (as though you were holding the ball of energy in front of you) and say: '**Please,** [your chosen higher 'beings of light'], **place in my hands all the energy that** [such-and-such] **took from me, and cleanse it completely . . .'** Imagine the energy, pristine white (and if you can't visualise anything, the process is working nonetheless). If you have children, add: '**If, in spite of myself, I have taken energy from my children** [say their names], **I return it to them, as I regain the energy that** [such-and-such] **took from me.'**

9. Slowly bring both hands to the centre of your chest, as if you were pressing a large ball against your breastbone. Take the time to appreciate this moment and say: '**I welcome these parts of my soul and will preserve them inside me.'**

10 Then say: '**Please,** [your chosen higher 'beings of light'], **allow** [such-and-such] **to take back the energy that other people** ['including me' if you think that you may have taken some of it] **have taken.'** To ensure that the restored energy doesn't get lost again, add: '**Before the witnesses** [your chosen higher 'beings of light'], **I order the ties of suffering** [and all the bad memories linked to them] **between** [such-and-such] **and me to be cut in this life and in all the others, so that only ties of peace remain.'** There are many ties between you, including the ties of suffering. Cut them. If you are able to visualise these things, you can even form your fingers into a scissor shape and make the gesture of cutting these ties of suffering.

11. Do the same again with another person who has taken energy from you, up to a maximum of three people, one after another. If you have found the first recovery emotionally disturbing and you are tired, limit yourself to one, and rest for at least two weeks before trying another series of soul recoveries.

12. Thank your chosen higher 'beings of light' and yourself. Welcome the new energy by resting and taking care of yourself. Acknowledge this moment as an important step towards your goal.

Possible Feelings After A Soul Recovery

Remember: this technique is practised without the physical presence of the other person, so it works very well with people who have already passed away. Thanks to the mirror neurons we discussed earlier, the very fact of imagining that the other person is sitting opposite us makes them real for your brain. If you don't know your abuser's name, or what they look like (for example, because the events occurred when you were very young, or you aren't sure which person to visualise), adapt the technique like this: in parts 4, 6, 8, and 10, say 'the person who did [fill in the hurtful act] to me . . .'

You can use this method in relation to anybody who has taken energy from you, beginning with the first person who repeatedly destabilised you (perhaps your father, mother, brother or sister) and continuing with others from your romantic, social or professional relationships. If you have a doubt about a certain relationship, it's important to trust your instinct. If you feel *lost* in the face of a certain person's actions or silences, it means you have *lost* a part of your energy as a result of this relationship. Practise the technique. It's normal to experience different feelings between each *energy recovery*. When you bring the *ball of energy* back towards you, your feelings will also vary. You can reclaim your energy from several people one after another, or focus on one each time. It's up to you.

If you feel tired, or experience slight pain anywhere in the body in the evening or when you wake up, don't worry. This liberation has changed the energy inside you, and your body needs to rebalance itself without resorting to the 'crutches' that it has relied on for so many years. Go out for a walk, get close to nature, take a bath, have an early night, seek out beauty, laugh and say thank you to life.

Rest assured, these slight pains will pass and everything will find its place. If you sleep badly the night after an energy recovery, it means that the process has brought back painful memories that need to be expelled. It's highly advisable to carry out the task of reconstruction with the help of short therapies such as EFT, EMDR, massage, acupuncture or magnetizm. A few sessions will help to expel the painful emotions. In other words, if the techniques are used in conjunction with therapy, a line can well and truly be drawn under those past painful experiences.

It's important to carry out these techniques several times for each person who has destabilised you. The first time, you might stumble over your words and need to read them from the page, or you might not express yourself forcefully enough. The second time, a fortnight or a month later (having allowed your body time to assimilate the process), you will be more familiar with the exercise and will do it with more conviction. The third time, you'll know it by heart and your intention will be far more powerful, making the positive effects on your life easy to see. And don't forget to listen to your feelings. When you have practised these techniques several times over a long period, you will experience feelings of liberating joy.

The following example shows the effectiveness of repeating these rituals. A young woman who had been harassed by her brother since childhood told me that the first time she practised the technique, the dictatorial emails from her brother stopped. The second time, her fear diminished and they were able to talk face-to-face, in a normal way. The third time, he apologised to her. She added: 'Things are gradually settling down, and it seems almost miraculous to have such a powerful technique, which works invisibly and yet has direct repercussions on my relationships.'

This process of exchange allows the 'energy thief' to change as well as the victim, depending on how receptive the thief is to change. If he or she has agreed to work on their problems with a therapist, there is a chance that having the missing part of their soul returned to them will be enough to open their eyes to their harmful actions. In the case of narcissistic abusers this is rare, but I have encountered several such cases. It's important to acknowledge this potential for improvement, because we're often told that they are incurable. As a rule, a person takes someone else's energy because their own energy was taken when they were young, and the compensatory cycle continues. For example, a parent takes energy from their child to fill a gap that someone else opened up in them. If a parent takes their child's energy, it doesn't necessarily mean that they are a narcissistic abuser, it may simply be that they have suffered a lot, and have developed a 'vampire' attitude (developing over-intense relationships, humiliating others, voicing endless criticism). Practising these techniques means interrupting the cycle and repairing the circulation of energy.

Bear in mind that if a difficult emotion (connected to a manipulative situation) occasionally returns after the process of soul recovery, it simply means there are still some elements to reclaim. In that case, go through the technique again in relation to the same person. In the end, you will feel more tranquil and less fearful. People often tell me they no longer feel an emptiness inside them. Sometimes it can be a very physical sensation: some no longer feel constantly hungry, others experience deeper and more refreshing sleep. Becoming whole means discovering your true identity and reclaiming your full powers. You'll be surprised how good it feels to be back in the driving seat of your own life.

Now it's time to free yourself from certain behaviours that are the result of ordeals experienced by your parents and ancestors. The next stage is decisive in your quest for serenity. It changed my life.

Chapter 10

Your Emotional Inheritance

We have all seen how certain scenarios recur from one generation to the next. For example, if our grandmother lost her mother at a young age, we may not have a good relationship with our own mother; if our grandfather went bankrupt, our own business may run into financial trouble; if our mother was assaulted, we may have problematic relationships with men; if our aunt complained about having to bring up her children alone, we may struggle to have a child ourselves; if we have an uncle who was a Catholic priest, we may have trouble finding love. Not all of our difficulties can be explained by a link to our ancestors, of course, but if we are doing everything we can to attain our goal but success still inexplicably evades us, then the explanation may lie in 'cellular memory', or what psychogenealogists call the transgenerational burden.

This concept of emotional burdens inherited from our family is not a new one. Almost a hundred years ago, Freud described how an emotion could be transmitted from one generation to the next, linked to a fault that people are no longer aware of, and don't remember.* Jung, Françoise Dolto and Dr J. L. Moreno discuss the secrets and things left unsaid that create 'invisible loyalties' and leave us with a debt to pay to our

* *Totem and Taboo* (Routledge, 2001) [2nd edition]

ancestors. And – as we have already seen – the psychologist Anne Ancelin Schützenberger devoted twenty years to studying transgenerational inheritance in her clinical and social psychology laboratory at the University of Nice.*

Be Aware of Your Links to the Past

Just as we inherit physical traits (curly hair, green eyes), it seems that we can also inherit the 'undigested' ordeals of our ancestors. It's true that if we look carefully into our family history, we often discover ordeals that resemble our own. To avoid repetitive scenarios, we need to empty our emotional memory and release ourselves from ties to the past. Most existing techniques for doing this require the presence of a therapist, another person or a group, but I'm happy to propose a method that anyone can use alone, at any point in their life.

In 2014, I had just produced six films for the M6 TV channel in less than eighteen months, and I was hurt by the fact that nobody had acknowledged this. I felt invisible. I had a recognition problem.

What could be the explanation for this? I tried to find out if anyone in my family had previously struggled to gain professional recognition. My aunt was the first to spring to mind. She was a nun, and also a writer, and my parents had named me after her. The similarities seemed to end there, however, because she had been fully recognised for her work, both by her French readers and also abroad, in Canada, Spain and Brazil.

In fact, I had singled out the wrong person. I'd been looking for a similar professional scenario, when I actually needed to broaden my search to a more general *absence of recognition*. I

* See her book *The Ancestor Syndrome* (Routledge, 1998).

continued my investigations and, in June 2015, thanks to a passing comment made by a friend, I realised that I'd inherited an emotional burden from my grandmother: she used to toil on behalf of her family, her neighbours, her church, her village . . . and yet nobody talked about her. The idea that this generous woman, who never complained, could have passed this painful legacy on to me was difficult to understand, until I realised that she'd passed it on *without meaning to*.

How could I free myself from it? In September 2015, another friend suggested that I consult Jean-Pierre Hermans, an interior designer who is also a medium. I instinctively felt that he could help me. I explained my problem to him over the phone, and he immediately outlined a process for clearing away the ties of suffering. I am still grateful to him for this. That very evening, without telling anyone what I was doing, I put it into practice regarding my grandmother, who had died eleven years earlier. Imagine my surprise when, the next morning, I was invited to talk about my work on the radio by a broadcaster who had recently interviewed my husband. It wasn't that the media had suddenly changed their mind about my work, but that I had only just freed myself from a wound that didn't belong to me!

Every time I came up against an unexplained obstacle, I continued exploring these transgenerational ties, and over the years my awareness of this heritage increased. Only recently, I carried out the process recommended by Jean-Pierre Hermans in relation to my paternal grandfather, who had, I discovered, suffered in a similar way to me. This process of liberation from inheritance is outlined in the next chapter.

Let's take the time to think about difficulties you have experienced and compare them to your family's problems. It's disturbing to think that our lives can become part of an endless cycle that sometimes skips a generation, and can affect our children and grandchildren. No parent wants to pass on their wounds to their descendants – and in any case, they are usually unaware that they are doing so – but we must remember that our soul has selected our family members as having the potential to help us overcome our ordeals. These are the people best placed to allow us to heal our wounds, and we can continue exploring our family history for as long as it takes to complete this healing. There's no point resenting our family for having passed their ordeals down to us: they didn't possess the tools that you are about to acquire.

Becoming more aware of our heritage – by researching our family tree – is straightforward. It simply requires a small effort of memory to consider each member of your family. Sometimes, however, our mind hides the truth from us, making us unable to recognise recurring patterns. In such cases, don't hesitate to consult a therapist (a psychologist specialising in transgenerational therapy, or in 'family constellations') to help you.

The following examples show how important this emotional cleansing can be. Claudie, a friend of mine, complained that she kept falling in love with men who were unavailable. The first was a doctor who devoted all his time to work; the second was married, and kept hinting that he would leave his wife without ever doing so; the third, an artist, spent a lot of time travelling and refused to commit to a serious relationship. There were several others – all married. She told me that her mother had never loved her father, and had been in love with another man. In an effort to make this man jealous, she had begun an affair with his best friend, and soon discovered she was pregnant. Reluctantly, she stayed with Claudie's father, and fell into a sort of fatalistic depression: 'I haven't got the life I wanted, and it's all because of this pregnancy. I'd have preferred to remain childless.' Unconsciously, she passed her wound on to her daughter: Claudie, who was single and childless, was living her mother's 'dream'. Her body was telling her (through her endometriosis) that she could free herself from this emotional scenario that didn't belong to her.

Sometimes, the inheritance is more subtle. Emma came to one of my workshops because she was suffering from respiratory problems (mainly asthma). I talked to her about these invisible genealogical links and she was amazed to discover that she had the same middle name, Sophie, as her godmother, who had always suffered from pneumonia, as well as chronic asthma and bronchitis.

The Problem of Secrets

Every family has its secrets. They sometimes remain buried for generations, because people fear that they will cause upset. I'm often asked whether it's important to bring these secrets out into the open. We often keep a secret in order to protect our loved ones, especially our children. We keep silent to avoid shame, to avoid having to admit we've lied, because we're afraid of disappointing someone, because we don't know how to articulate something, or because we've promised not to tell. However, any secret is likely to have an impact on our life or that of our descendants. Knowing about the lives of our ancestors, and of people whose name we share or who have a specific link to us (godfather, godmother, etc.), allows us to understand the ordeals we are going through. Often, something that is a shameful secret for one generation is less shocking for the next. We can help our children by acknowledging, sincerely, that: 'In life, when we go through difficult experiences, we make mistakes.' By articulating the fact that the person responsible for the 'shameful' secret probably suffered a lot before making their mistake, we show that everyone has the right to be fallible. If, however, our children feel that we are judging someone, they will sense that we might judge them similarly harshly, and will learn to keep their own secrets.

This is why we should study the relationship our parents had with their parents, and with their siblings, and then examine our own relationships with family members: it allows us to assimilate this emotional heritage. Let's ask ourselves a few questions. Have we cut off all contact with our family? Are we constantly judging their behaviour? Are we jealous of one of our siblings? Have we grown apart from our parents? Have we drawn a veil over our problems rather than trying to solve them? If so, we are taking the risk that our children will eventually act in the same way. Wouldn't we prefer to do our very best to be forgiven for our mistakes? And wouldn't we like to do the same for our own parents?

This study is all the more important because if we feel that just one of our parents is responsible for all our misfortunes, we are likely to find ourselves in conflict with people of the same sex as that parent. By working on this relationship, and 'detoxifying' the emotional trauma experienced by – and with – this parent, we can finally stop reproducing this cycle of suffering in our lives.

If we can't manage to tell people close to us about a traumatic event, we can write a letter and leave it for them to read if they choose, making it clear that we are not yet ready to discuss it. The day will come when we are ready. In this way, we can avoid the trauma being revisited on our descendants.

Sometimes, without meaning to, our parents put us through the same ordeal that devastated them as children. This isn't done maliciously, of course: it is the result of a transgenerational burden. I once heard an interesting story about this: in the early twentieth century, a shipbuilder was posted to Dakar. His wife, who had just given birth to a daughter, Madeleine, followed her husband to Africa but, afraid that Madeleine might fall ill there, left her in the care of her grandmother in Dunkirk. Madeleine suffered a great deal from never having known her parents, who only returned to France ten years later. When the Second World War broke out, Madeleine was married and had three children. Needing to escape the German invaders, she and her husband left for the South of France with their oldest child and their newborn baby, but they left their unruly second daughter, Claire, behind with her grandmother. The young girl felt this abandonment keenly; why couldn't Madeleine understand that she was forcing her daughter to undergo the same ordeal that she had endured as a child?

If the wound (in this instance felt as abandonment) remains unhealed, it will reproduce itself, and be experienced by another member of the family. If Claire continues to resent her mother, not understanding that she is replaying a scenario endured by her grandmother (who didn't possess the *key* to free herself), this wound of abandonment may reappear in one of her children, grandchildren or nephews, who will also feel abandoned. This could continue until someone frees themselves and, potentially, the whole family line. Claire may have reason to think that she is the *least loved* of the three daughters because her parents made her undergo this trauma alone, but we shouldn't forget that we ourselves have *chosen* our parents for the ordeals that will allow us to heal our soul. Should we blame them for what we have come to seek in this life: to repair ourselves, and free ourselves from our greatest ordeals? Are our siblings responsible for something that we lack, when in fact our soul has chosen this place in the family?

The traumatic event recurs in the strongest child, or the one most able to heal the wound.

Let's not waste time feeling guilty for having taken so long to feel more charitable towards our parents and wider family. We didn't know about the challenges we faced, and there is still time to put things right. Now, let's set ourselves free.

Chapter 11

Free at Last!

Freeing yourself from your transgenerational inheritance is straightforward with this technique, which you can use in relation to:

- Deceased people (and animals) whose deaths have left you feeling very sad.

- Very kind members of your family (living or deceased) from whom you have inherited an ordeal, a health problem or an emotional wound.

- All those who, through recurring illnesses within the family, have imposed 'limiting' beliefs on you (such as: 'men die at fifty-five years old', 'women get cancer').

- Relatives with whom you have experienced conflict or misunderstanding; you may want to cleanse your links to them, or simply release yourself from the anxiety of the situation.

- Your children, if you want to have a more peaceful relationship with them.

If the person has taken energy from you (sometimes unknowingly) by destabilising you, as parents sometimes do when they are suffering, the following technique won't be sufficient: you will need to carry out techniques 6 and 8 instead.

Personally, I cleansed my links to my grandmother, and a professional burden was immediately lifted. I did the same with my aunt, whose name I share, to avoid inheriting a difficult love life, and with my parents, from whom I inherited a few ordeals and wounds. I also practised this technique in relation to people with whom I'd been in conflict, and my relationships with almost all of them were vastly improved. While communication is still tricky with some of these people, I've been able to create a healthy distance between myself and the situation, with all its painful memories. It's a great relief.

Cleansing Your Ties of Suffering

Technique 7 is the only one you can practise in relation to your children, with the aim of easing your relationship. Your child can also do it in relation to a parent, if necessary, as long as they understand its meaning, undertake it voluntarily, and are self-motivated and mature.

You can memorise the steps involved, record them on your smartphone (leaving pauses to repeat the phrases) or you can read them with the book beside you.

TECHNIQUE 7

Freeing yourself from emotional inheritance

In order for this technique to be entirely effective, you must practise technique 5 (soul recovery following a shock) and technique 6 (soul recovery following an energy theft) beforehand, in relation to all the people who may have reduced your energy. Take the time to reread the whole of Chapter 9.

1. Choose a peaceful place, sit on a chair and place another one opposite you. Summon your powerful witnesses, the two higher 'beings of light' who will ensure that the steps proceed as they should (see technique 5, step 2). With your eyes open or closed, imagine their presence, their love and their goodwill surrounding you. If you can't imagine this, continue anyway, and the process will still work.

2. Summon the person with whom you have argued or whose emotional ordeals you no longer want to carry, and imagine that they are sitting down opposite you. Say out loud: '**Please**, [your chosen 'beings of light'], **invite** [such-and-such] **to sit down opposite me.**'

3. Now, tell them out loud what is on your mind. If it is an animal or a person you didn't know well, or someone who was always kind to you, say: '**I don't hold anything against you and I loved you very much; you are here because I want to free my painful emotions.**' In the case of an emotional inheritance, add: '**Your wound of** [state the wound] **and your ordeals** [say which] **are replaying themselves in my life** [say how]. **These are your ordeals and your wounds; I am freeing myself from them just as you can. By freeing yourself from your burdens, you can help me.**' Example: 'You were unhappy in love, you didn't follow your dream career, and your brother stole your inheritance. You

experienced all these things as injustices, and I am also experiencing injustice with my partner. It's over: this ordeal and this injustice belong to you, and I am freeing myself from them just as you can free yourself.' For a deceased person whose death saddens you, say: '**Your death causes me pain. Go towards the light to be in peace, and help me find peace.**'

4. Remain silent. Each of your thoughts is actually a response from the other: you may sense gratitude, bringing tears to your eyes. When nothing else comes, it means that the other person has finished. If no thoughts come, it means the person agrees with you.

5. Next, say to them: '**You've heard me, I've heard you. Before the witnesses** [name the chosen higher 'beings of light'], **I ask that the ties of suffering between** [such-and-such] **and me (as well as the emotional inheritance that belongs to you) be completely cleansed and freed from all suffering, in this life and in all the others, so that only ties of love remain.**'

Professor Linus Pauling, recipient of both the Nobel Peace Prize and the Nobel Prize in Chemistry, wrote: 'Life results due to a relationship of molecules and is not a property of any one molecule.' In the light of this, we can see why even a distant family member can have an impact on our health, as the following example shows.

Nelly is a nurse in Douarnenez, Brittany. The newborn baby of one of her colleagues was in hospital, being operated on for pyloric stenosis (he was regurgitating after drinking). Nelly spoke to me on the very day she'd put this technique into practice: 'I'd attended one of your workshops, and had become aware of the effect of family ties,' she said. 'I asked my colleague if anyone in her family had previously suffered this same problem, and she said that her uncle had. So I plucked up my courage and told her to tell her baby that this was not his problem and that he should have confidence in himself because he could free himself from it. She did that, and this evening the baby seems better. He drank his bottle and kept the milk down. He seems calmer. I'm amazed, because even yesterday morning I wouldn't have been able to make that connection.'

Cut Your Toxic Ties

There was still one dark cloud in my life. Many years earlier, a man I knew had launched an attack on my family that had destabilised our already fragile balance still further. He was motivated by frustrated love, and his actions had left me devastated. Of course, he said it was all my fault. I alternated between hatred and a desire for revenge. At that point, cleansing the ties of suffering with him was completely out of the question for me. I was nowhere near being ready to begin that process. That was the state of mind I found myself in when my younger sister suddenly fell into a coma following a ruptured aneurysm. A second was all it took for her to lose consciousness completely. I had already been through something similar when I'd travelled to Afghanistan with my husband, and his brother was killed in a car accident almost in front of our very eyes. I'd already lost my grandparents, some uncles, aunts, and even friends, but this time it was my sister. I was overwhelmed with helplessness, rage and sadness, and the frustrations of my day-to-day life suddenly seemed trivial. All the time she was in a coma, during my visits to her, and right up until she passed away, I became aware of an ever-present anger directed against this man that I was nurturing inside me. This feeling was holding me in a constant state of resentment, and casting a shadow over my horizon. I had to free myself from it, but how? I remembered the technique of cleansing the ties of suffering, and another more *determined* version. When it comes to toxic relationships, we don't *ask*, we *order*. We don't *cleanse* the ties of suffering, we *cut* them. We don't choose *love* as our end goal, but *peace*.

When I put it into practice, I had the physical sensation of a weight lifting from my body. I knew I had reached a decisive moment in my life, successfully breaking the vicious cycle that had locked us into endless conflict. I owe this journey towards serenity to the sister I lost.

This technique can be practised in relation to:

- Your biological parents, if you were abandoned.

- People (living or deceased) who have taken energy from you and caused you suffering (practise technique 6 beforehand).

- Members of your family, living or deceased, from whom you have inherited an ordeal, a health problem or an emotional wound, and who have taken energy from you, thus destabilising you or causing you suffering (practise technique 6 beforehand).

TECHNIQUE 8

Cutting the ties of suffering

If somebody (living or deceased) has taken energy from you and caused you suffering by criticising you, mistreating you or humiliating you, or if they have destabilised you with their silences, unpredictable behaviour, tears, anger or violence (physical, mental or sexual), you must first practise technique 6 in relation to them. In this case, please go directly to stage 3.

1. The beginning is the same (see technique 5, stage 2): choose somewhere peaceful, take two chairs, invite two higher 'beings of light' to assist you and imagine their benevolent presence around you (if you can't imagine this, it doesn't matter, the process will still work).

2. Summon the person with whom you have experienced conflict and say out loud: '**Please,** [your two chosen higher 'beings of light'], **order** [such-and-such] **to sit down opposite me.**' If you don't know the person's name, you can simply say 'the person who did this to me'.

3. Tell them what is troubling you, and unburden yourself. If you are addressing parents, grandparents, uncles or aunts, take the chance to free yourself from their emotional burdens by saying: '**Your wound of** [state the wound] **and your ordeals** [say which] **are replaying themselves in my life** [say how]. **These are your ordeals and your wounds; I am freeing myself from them just as you can.**' For example: 'You have passed the violence you suffered at the hands of your father down to me. I don't want to carry this burden any more; I am freeing myself from it just as you can free yourself.'

4. Remain silent. Each of your thoughts is actually a response from the other. When nothing else comes, it means that the other person has finished. If no thoughts come, it means the person agrees with you.

> 5. Next, say out loud and with a powerful intention: 'You heard me, I heard you. Before the witnesses [name the chosen higher 'beings of light'], I order that the ties of suffering between [such-and-such] and me (as well as the emotional inheritance that belongs to you) be cut, in this life and in all the others, so that only ties of peace remain.'

There are, of course, other techniques that work in a similar way to this one, but the advantage of this one is that we have two powerful *allies* who help us through it. Their support will be invaluable if the other person puts up any form of resistance.

Bear in mind that you haven't cut all ties, simply the ties of suffering. This is important, especially for those who are practising the technique in relation to a parent or sibling. As with all the techniques, speak out loud and don't hesitate to repeat things several times in order to emphasise the intention. The second time, you will feel more confident. The third time, the energy with which you recite the phrases will produce better results. Repeat the process every time the problems recur and, when you feel freed from the weight of this relationship, you can practise the ritual in relation to another person, if need be.

This technique is a language spoken between one soul and another. The other person is not physically present, but a part of them has heard us. Sometimes, this has a big impact on the relationship between the people concerned, and we may be surprised to observe changes in the other person's behaviour. In other cases, the only impact is on ourselves, but we are no longer wounded by the other person's actions and we are less fearful of them. Personally, I noticed that my dislike and resentment

evaporated, making my life considerably easier. It had an imme-
diate effect on my relationships with those around me. The
ordeals receded into the distance: I had freed myself.

If a technique doesn't work, there can be several explanations.
Did you carry out (and repeat a fortnight later) the soul recovery after a shock (technique 5)? And did you do the same for
technique 6? You may have forgotten to do it in relation to
somebody. Sometimes the list of people is long: father, mother,
brother, sister, ex-partner, colleagues, friends . . . Take the time
to reread the whole of Chapter 9 slowly. It's difficult to create
distance between you and the recurring cycle of ordeals. Don't
hesitate to ask advice from a friend or therapist about the
recurrence of this emotional inheritance among you and your
family members.

To free yourself from the ties of suffering, you can make use
of two techniques:

- *Technique 7 cleanses the tie with a relative (living or
  deceased) in order to be free from a transgenerational
  inheritance and no longer carry the weight of their ordeals.
  Think about your names, as these can indicate people with
  whom you may have ties that need cleansing. (Don't make
  the mistake of believing that in choosing certain names for
  your children you have made them inherit an emotional
  burden from their ancestors. Emotional inheritance occurs
  no matter what people's names are, and giving your
  children a name that is shared with others in your family is
  actually an advantage, as it may help them with the process
  of freeing themselves in the future). You can also cleanse
  the ties with people you know (friends, colleagues, lovers)
  in order to free yourself of their resentment, disagreements*

*and conflicts, and to ensure that you don't make them
experience the effects of your own wounds in return.*

- *Technique 8 cuts the ties of suffering in cases of
  relationships that are conflictual, inappropriate (a parent
  who expects their child to behave like an adult) or toxic
  (hypercritical, abusive or humiliating, characterised by
  anger, silences, unpredictable behaviour, tears or physical/
  mental/emotional violence).*

- *Adopted children can practise these techniques with their
  adoptive family, because the cycle of ordeals recurs in the
  same way. Don't forget that our soul chooses our relatives
  in order to replay the same wounds until they are healed.*

- *Allow yourself to absorb the techniques. Pause between
  each series of steps, progressing carefully and without haste.*

Let's finish with one last example: at a conference in Belgium,
I was once approached by a couple in their sixties. The husband
spoke first: 'You can't imagine how happy we are to have learned
about this technique. My mother-in-law is horrible, and she sent
my wife away when she was little.' His wife wiped away tears
and added: 'She sent me away to boarding school, but kept my
brothers at home. I wasn't allowed to go home until I was married. She's toxic. My older sister died when she was only a few
days old, and another sister who was born soon after me also
died. Even our three little female kittens died. Now my own
daughters resent me for not letting them get to know their
grandmother. Even today, she still behaves very badly towards
me. I'm going to try this technique and I hope it will put an end
to all this. I never want to hear from her again.'

Her anger was palpable, and as I listened to her an idea
began to form in my mind. My instincts sometimes tell me

unexpected things, but I always listen to them, so I said to this woman: 'Could the house where your family lived have been a hostile environment for anything young and female?' (This phenomenon has been described by the biologist Rupert Sheldrake, who demonstrated the existence of 'morphic fields' that contain recurring information, which he calls 'collective memory'. This is also known as the 'memory of walls', when the information is linked to events that occurred in the home.) 'Perhaps your mother, rather than expelling you from the family, removed you from a place that killed your sisters and your kittens? It would have been unconscious, of course, but she may have done you the greatest favour of all: she saved your life by removing you from a house that had the power to harm you. As soon as you were a young woman, you were permitted to return.' The woman began to tremble and covered her mouth with her hand: 'What you're saying really resonates with me. I've always thought I could never forgive her, but now I know I can.'

I've lost count of the number of people who have told me that just reading about this technique gave them a palpable sense of relief even before they carried it out, as though the process of healing had already begun. I'm convinced that as soon as I began to describe this procedure during my talk, this woman began to assimilate the ritual, paving the way for this rapid change in attitude. When we are freed from our wounds, our hatred and anger dissipate.

Chapter 12

Removing Your Blockages

S tep by step, you are progressing towards your own healing. You have cleansed yourself of your emotional burdens, and you are no longer carrying a load that does not belong to you. Better still, you have now managed to identify your wounds, and seal up the cracks they caused. After so many ordeals, you are standing tall, a different, stronger person. Your life has taken a positive turn and your whole attitude has changed. You no longer see yourself as a victim of other people or of life in general. Many of your troubles have evaporated, so you may be finding it hard to understand why certain blockages remain. Note down anything that isn't fluid, any dreams that you haven't managed to fulfil, and anything in your life that isn't progressing as you would like it to:

– _____

– _____

– _____

– _____

– _____

– _____

These obstacles may spring from emotional inheritances or feelings of guilt stemming from your childhood.

Detaching Yourself from Inherited Blockages

In order to eliminate blockages relating to your family, identify them (professional, financial, family, romantic) and determine whether they stem from:

- a lack of recognition from others;

- a lack of space in your relationship with your partner, in your family or in your professional life (for example, if you can't manage to exist on your own terms, and feel *invisible*, or as though you are in somebody else's shade);

- a problem of legitimacy (in your own eyes): you don't give yourself the right to be happy, successful or proud.

Now, note down the main failures, difficult experiences and ordeals suffered by your parents, grandparents and those who share your name.

- _____

- _____

- _____

- _____

- _____

- _____

Compare these to your own ordeals, and identify any recurring cycles, then cleanse the ties of suffering with these people using technique 7.

The blockages we experience in our daily lives can spring from a feeling of guilt. Guilt can be a harmful sensation, and can crop up at any time and obstruct our progress, even when we are achieving all sorts of successes.

No More Guilt!

Some temperaments are more inclined than others to experience guilt. Personally, I think I must have been a St Bernard in a former life, one of those big shaggy dogs that were used to help locate people lost in the mountains, and are still pictured with a little barrel of brandy around their necks. Like them, I can't stand seeing anybody suffer – I'm burdened with extra-strength triple-absorbency empathy. This tendency to feel guilty for other people's suffering has been increased by the presence of people in my life who have always told me that everything is my fault. And I must admit, I was always very ready to believe it!

The process is well known: when we feel guilty, others realise this, and are quick to accuse us. The result is inevitable: without knowing it, we *punish* ourselves by refusing to allow ourselves those things that we all aspire to: love, happiness, recognition and success. And believing that we deserve success is no guarantee that we will achieve it: there are powerful forces at work inside us, hampering everything we do. I have observed that people who complain that their lives don't live up to their expectations often harbour deep feelings of guilt. Let's explore the five main scenarios that produce such feelings.

1. *We have let down a friend (or we think we have)*
   We have lied, lost our temper, or forgotten something that meant a lot to the other person, or even deceived them unintentionally. We have neglected someone, or think we have, or haven't kept our promises (to look for work, to give up drinking . . .).

2. *We have failed to help somebody (including ourselves)*
   For example, we have been absent, neglected to say something that needed to be said, given bad advice, remained passive in the face of mistreatment, or felt powerless when a friend was suffering.

3. *We have caused somebody's death (or we think we have)*
   If there has been an accident caused by our own error or negligence, or if we have had to make a choice to save one person (including ourselves) and sacrifice another, if our mother died giving birth to us, or if we have kept a secret in order to protect someone and that secret has destroyed another person's life.

4. *We have received more than somebody else, or we have hurt someone when trying to help them*
   If we are particularly favoured by somebody, if we have received more than our fair share, if we think our happiness and success will cause another to suffer, or if we are the only survivor of a terrible accident.

5. *We have intentionally hurt someone*
   We have behaved badly towards someone because we wanted to cause them pain, because we have acted selfishly, or because we ourselves were suffering, and now we are consumed with remorse.

How can we free ourselves from our guilt? We simply need to reconnect with someone we all know, but whom we tend to overlook: our inner 'child'. This part of ourselves began life bursting with enthusiasm and curiosity, but it has been damaged over the course of time by hurtful comments and a series of ordeals. We are going to identify the moment when a shadow fell across our faces, in order to bring back a light that will chase the shadows away. These moments may often seem trivial, without obvious consequences, and those around us might not recognise them as being at the root of our unhappiness. We are the only ones who can know the distress they caused.

Note down any feelings of guilt you have felt during your life, at any age, in any order.

- _____

- _____

- _____

- _____

- _____

- _____

Circle the feeling that causes you most pain. If it's linked to a current situation, it's likely to be the aftershock of an upheaval that occurred much earlier in your life. Try to identify a painful scenario in your childhood that caused you to feel similar guilt. Go back as far as you can – you need to find the very first instance of it. If you can't remember clearly, consult a kinesiologist. Kinesiology shifts the focus from the mental to the physical using muscular reflexes, and allows your body to speak by asking it:

how old was I when I experienced my first feelings of guilt? This will help your memories to resurface.

Comfort Your Inner 'Child'

Have you identified the incident that sparked your feeling of guilt? Then it's time to get rid of that feeling. How can this be done? I suggest that you use an approach that has something in common with hypnosis, in that you 'revisit' the past in order to modify the incident in question for good. Remember that, thanks to our mirror neurons, our brains don't differentiate between a real situation and an imagined exercise, as long as we perceive the exercise to be real. By allowing our intention to make use of our imagination, we can put an end to the influence our painful souvenirs have over us.

TECHNIQUE 9

Our consolation

1. You have identified a major cause of guilt. If you have identified more than one, focus on the one that occurred earliest, even if it seems less important. Imagine yourself today as a 'Big You', talking to a 'Little You' (this is you at the age when the painful incident occurred). Put your name after 'Little' or 'Big'. For example, I would say, 'Big Natacha is with Little Natacha.' Rather like an adult looking after a child in trouble, 'Big You' approaches in a spirit of goodwill, giving 'Little You' a cuddle.

2. In your imagination, 'Big You' takes 'Little You' by the hand and leads the way to the exact time and place where you experienced this guilt as a child. The person who gave rise

to this feeling is present in your thoughts, as though they were really there.

3. Recount the events aloud, as though you are reliving them. As the guilt makes its appearance, ask yourself: 'What would I have liked to do? How would I have liked the other person to react, and what would I have wanted them to say?' Imagine what the other person could have done in order for you not to have felt guilty (even if this seems inconceivable) and tell this improved story. This version needs to be much more pleasant, so that 'Little You' is no longer hurt by it.

If you have hurt somebody, whether intentionally or due to negligence, selfishness or your own suffering, 'Little You' asks for forgiveness from 'Big You' for the causes of this guilt. 'Little You' thanks 'Big You' for having allowed them to become aware of their acts.

4. After having told this ideal version of the story, 'Big You' reassures 'Little You' by discussing the event with the benefit of hindsight. Forgive 'Little You', using a very strong intention. For example, you could say:

- 'You did your best, given your age.'

- 'If you'd known, you'd have acted differently.'

- 'Everybody makes mistakes. That's how we learn.'

- 'You reacted that way because you felt threatened or neglected.'

- 'You were too young to understand the other person's attitude.'

- 'It's not your fault you received more than (such-and-such). His/her soul *chose* their place among the siblings in order to learn from these ordeals.'

- 'That person died because it was their time. In some way, I had to experience this ordeal in order to progress along my soul path.'

- 'I was clumsy, I acted badly, or said terrible things to (such-and-such), but now I've changed and I apologise.'

  Don't forget that the souls of your children, your siblings and your parents (the family members with whom you experienced this guilt) chose to be incarnated in this family in order to get over certain ordeals.

5. 'Big You' ends by saying out loud to 'Little You': 'You came into this world in order to learn from your mistakes and your ordeals, and you will carry some essential things with you through life. You must forgive yourself: you deserve to be loved and you have the right to be happy. The happier you are, the more you will inspire joy in those around you. I will always be there for you, without judging you. You no longer need to rely on the judgement of others in order to progress. You have never disappointed me and I will always look after you. I accept you just as you are. I love you unconditionally and forever.'

Remember, your 'Big You' needs to convince your 'Little You' that they aren't alone and that they will always be loved unconditionally. It's important to find the words to repair the unhappiness and anger, the fear of doing wrong, the unease, the guilt, the shame, the feelings of abandonment, and the anxiety of this child who has suffered a lot. For this part, you don't need to learn the phrases off by heart – be spontaneous. If you find yourself tearful, it's further proof of liberation.

If you don't feel able to do this exercise alone, you can seek the help of a therapist specialising in hypnosis, somatotherapy, EFT, EMDR or sophrology (all techniques that focus on managing the emotions). They will help you through this process of calling on 'Big You' and 'Little You'.

The following examples show how guilt can impede our actions and have an impact on all sorts of areas of our lives.

Lack of Professional Success

Chloé is a specialist in personal development. It's well known that we can excel at advising others but be less successful when it comes to ourselves, and Chloé found herself engulfed by a sense of guilt that was affecting her wellbeing and the book she wrote two years ago. She asked me for help, and we established that the memory of this emotion went back to when she was four years old. Her father had just bought a tube of glue and had set it down on an antique table. Full of curiosity, Chloé ran over to the table, opened the glue and spilled a few drops on the table. When her parents realised what she'd done they gave her a severe telling-off, criticising her for being so curious. It may seem like a trivial incident, but reliving it was very painful for Chloé; she was in tears as she told me about it. I asked her to imagine Big Chloé (as she is now) taking Little Chloé (at four years old) by the hand and asking her to tell the story right up to the fateful moment. Then, we had the following conversation:

'What would you have liked your parents to say when they discovered the glue on the table?'

'That it didn't matter . . .'

'That's not enough to put it right. Imagine them apologising for having hurt you.'

'Oh, they'd never do that. They were very strict, even towards themselves.'

'What would you have liked them to say, even if it's not the sort of thing they'd normally say?'

Then, Chloé imagined her father talking to Little Chloé: 'It doesn't matter, we'll clean it all off. We're sorry we hurt you, and I apologise for reacting that way.' In this ideal scenario, her mother added: 'It's good to be curious, it's a joyful thing. We love you and you don't need to worry. We learn from our mistakes.' I asked her to visualise her parents giving her a big hug. Then she said this to Little Chloé: 'I love you unconditionally, whatever you do and whatever mistakes you make. I will never judge you and I will always be by your side. You have a right to be happy and successful.' Two weeks later, I saw on Facebook that her book was suddenly receiving lots of good reviews from readers, even though it had been published two years earlier. Chloé became noticeably happier, and her editor commissioned her to write two more books soon afterwards. Her sense of guilt had left her, and she could progress more serenely through life.

The Right to Happiness

Josselin was constantly needing to take time off work because of disease: stomach bugs, colds, migraines . . . and sometimes he found himself worrying about symptoms that disappeared as soon as he was given sick leave. He loved his job, and couldn't understand why he kept falling ill. When he analysed his own sense of guilt, he realised that he felt as though he was letting his boss down. In order to get rid of this feeling, he looked back into his childhood, right back to when he first experienced this sense of letting down a figure of *authority*. He soon remembered the event in question: one day, when he was six and his mother was in hospital following an operation, his father asked him to keep an eye on a pan of soup on the hob because he needed to pop back to his office. His father was away longer than expected, and eventually Josselin began to worry. He left the kitchen to look through the living room window and see if his father was on his way. The soup boiled over and Josselin, wanting to put things right, tried to wipe it up with a cloth that immediately caught fire. Very quickly, part of the kitchen was destroyed, and when his father arrived he was extremely angry.

Josselin told me that his father had needed to take on a lot of extra work to pay for the new kitchen, so his reaction, as a child, had been: 'If I didn't exist, this would never have happened. He wouldn't have had to work so hard – it's all my fault.' This feeling still affects him: part of him has been blocked since the age of six, trapped with the child who feels responsible for his father having to work himself to exhaustion.

Ever since then, Josselin has been *punishing himself* by attracting situations (diseases) that intrude on his happiest times. He decided to carry out the technique described above, and Big Josselin explained to Little Josselin that he felt guilty because of his father's anger. He told him that it wasn't his fault and that he should never have been left alone at the age of six. 'You did what you did because you were worried, and that was perfectly reasonable.' Big Josselin asked Little Josselin: 'How would you have wanted your father to react?' and the boy replied: 'I would have liked him not to shout, to say sorry for having kept me waiting, and to tell me it wasn't my fault.' Josselin then said the words that he wished his father had said: 'It's fine – the kitchen was ugly anyway, and now we'll be able to get a new one. Mum will be delighted! I'm sorry I've caused you so much hurt by being away a lot, and by my reaction. I apologise: I didn't realise that you were also very scared. I love you very much.' Since then, Josselin has stopped falling ill and has continued his career without interruptions.

This exercise focusing on our early feelings of guilt cleanses us of subsequent similar feelings, which are resurgences of the first wound. If we still feel painful traces of guilt, we can revisit later incidents in the same way, in order to complete the process.

A Health Problem

Laurent enjoys his job and is happy with his life in general. Six months ago, he began to work on his wound of rejection. He had realised that he needed to stop making himself and those around him relive this wound. Around the same time, he was puzzled to discover a patch of red skin on his chest, near his heart, which looked like an early manifestation of eczema. I suggested that he should look back at the events that had occurred just before the red patch appeared. He remembered an argument with his sister, during which she had criticised him harshly and refused to engage in any kind of cordial dialogue. I suggested that he should try to remember any older examples of guilty feelings that had also resulted in a sense of rejection, but he couldn't recall anything. However, he did tell me a story that his family had often told him, to everyone's amusement: when his younger sister was born, every time his parents were busy with her he would do something naughty. So, Big Laurent spoke to Little Laurent, and reassured him, saying: 'I will always be there for you and I will always look after you, even when our parents can't. I will never reject you. You don't need the approval of others, and I love you unconditionally, whatever you do.' That very evening, the skin problem receded, and after three days it had gone, without the need for medication.

If you can't remember an event in your childhood that sparked guilty feelings, think about the funny stories your family tell about you, without realising that they may conceal a wound of guilt. What terms do your family use to describe you when you were a child?

A Lack of Recognition and Wellbeing

Gérard is a human resources manager in a big company. He's a high-achieving man who earns a good living, but deep down he regrets not having fulfilled his dream to work for a big multinational company abroad. A few months before he was due to retire, he became seriously ill, despite having been in excellent health until then. When he looked into his past for old wounds of guilt, he realised that he felt responsible for the death of his cousin, who had been hit by a car while they'd played together as children. He realised that he had always seen to the needs of others before his own, and that he had *punished* himself by not fulfilling all his ambitions. Now, his health problem was depriving him of the freedom and happiness that his retirement should bring. In order to free himself, Big Gérard said to Little Gérard: 'If you were the one who had died, would you want your cousin to be sad, and not allow himself to be happy? Of course not. So go and be happy. You're not responsible for his death, and remember: his soul decided to pass on.' In this case, Gérard had to carry out the technique several times before the guilt fully disappeared. He then began to look forward to a healthy and happy retirement. Ironically, three months before the date he had set, one of his old employers finally offered him a job running a big NGO abroad.

You can carry out the same exercise, with Big You and Little You, revisiting and improving a past event. You can do it in relation to any unpleasant emotion: anger, frustration, shame, fear, anxiety. You simply need to look back to your childhood and identify the first time you experienced this emotion, then imagine you are reliving it today. As you do this, look after yourself, reassure yourself, comfort yourself, and repeat phrases that will repair the damage, just as you would with a child you love.

By rewriting the story of the event that gave rise to our guilty feeling, our mind ceases to see this story as a trauma. This return to the past may only last a few minutes, but it frees us forever from the scenarios that were holding us back, and consoles us for the rest of our life.

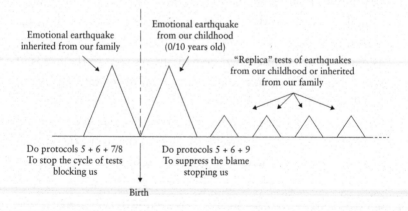

Chapter 13

The Secret Power of Forgiveness

There's one point on which all personal development manuals agree: the importance of forgiveness. This means forgiving others, of course, but also forgiving ourselves. When I began to look into the idea of forgiveness, I initially thought of it as a fashionable concept, mingling Buddhist and Judeo-Christian thinking. Apart from its moral value, I didn't attach much importance to it, and I also didn't think I had anything to forgive myself for.

However, my long period of self-exploration completely changed my mind. I discovered the significance of ordeals I'd experienced, and understood that they were part of endless cycles triggered by wounds inherited from my childhood or my ancestors. I realised that my soul had drawn me to these challenging people and situations to give me the chance to free myself from them. If I had never come up against chaotic situations or suffered difficult setbacks, would I ever have sought to rebuild myself? Would I have tried to heal my wounds and strengthen my weak points? My family, my friends, my partner, my colleagues: they were all sources of conflict but, equally, the *witnesses* my soul was seeking in order to show me what I needed to repair. In many ways, these people allowed me to free myself. As for my anger and resentment, I learned that these toxic feelings destroy those who feel them far more quickly than those who cause them. Resentment doesn't nourish us, it devours us. Finally, thanks to the various techniques, I stopped seeing people as 'bad', and recognised their suffering. I was no longer a victim and they were no longer persecutors. Together, we were the solution!

After that, my ordeals turned into experiences, and I was able to practise forgiveness because I loved the person I'd become, the person I'd rebuilt in the wake of these painful experiences. I'm now stronger than I've ever been, and I owe it to this freedom. Can we really resent the people who have allowed us to achieve serenity, happiness and success? Of course not! I now understand the value of forgiveness.

Forgiving others is important, but we also need to forgive ourselves. Given that my soul drew these painful events towards it, I am partly responsible for the initial upheavals I suffered and their subsequent reiterations. That is why I accepted the need to forgive myself, by forgiving my soul for having made me endure so many ordeals.

The True Secret of Forgiveness

I didn't know it then, but I still had an important discovery to make. Understanding the true value of forgiveness was a revelation. On 1 January 2017, my mother called to tell me that my father had been rushed to hospital with **pneumonia** and might not survive the night. Her words hit me like a blow to the chest. 'I'm on my way!' I said. As I threw some things into a bag, I thought about the symbolism of this disease: pneumonia can indicate discouragement, a feeling of being in the way, or worry that there may not be a solution to our problems. What could have happened to my father? About a week earlier, the family had come together for the funeral of his brother-in-law. Perhaps there was a link, but what could it be? This death had been a result of old age, and it was in the natural order of things.

Stéphane, my husband, came to the hospital with me, and I admitted to him that I couldn't understand what was happening. I blamed myself, because two days earlier my father had been suffering from a persistent, whistling cough. Trusting my intuition, I'd carried on as though nothing was wrong, telling myself that I shouldn't worry and that everything would come right. How had I been so blind? In the lift down to intensive care, I asked Stéphane to stay with my mother so that I could talk to my father and identify the emotional upheaval that had caused his pneumonia. I went into the room and had to hide my shock. He was lying on a bed with machines all around him that beeped every few seconds. His heart rate and blood pressure were being tracked on little screens, and they were both frighteningly high. He was being given oxygen and had a drip in his arm. He was very pale, and I could see a frightened glint in his half-closed eyes. Despite my mother's alarm over the phone, I was still shocked. She clung on to us, glad not to be alone any more.

'Natacha will stay here – you need to get some fresh air. I'll come with you,' Stéphane said to my mother.

I sat down on the bed beside my father. Where to start?

'Tell me what's bothering you, Dad . . .'

'It hurts. I can't breathe,' he said, his voice barely audible.

'I understand, but is there something making you sad?'

He was silent for a moment, before replying.

'This isn't the first time I've had pneumonia. I had it when I was two, but my older brother saved my life by donating blood to me because I was so weak. If it hadn't been for him . . .'

He left his sentence unfinished, and a tear ran down his cheek. His older brother had died a few years earlier. I encouraged him to carry on, so he told me a sad story that had been a secret until then. He had always felt extremely angry with his own father and mother, who had abandoned him at the age of fifteen and had left him in the care of his older sister and . . . her husband, Maurice! The man we had buried a week earlier had looked after him like a father. An image formed itself in my mind: Maurice was holding something in his hand – one of the veils that my father had placed over his childhood pain. Like a cloth that slips from a table when we tug it, this veil had disappeared with death, leaving my father exposed to a reality that had left him devastated so many years ago. Maurice's death had reactivated a painful memory (the feeling of being a burden) lodged in my father's unconscious, causing his immune system to break down. I saw that we needed to cleanse the ties of suffering between him and his parents, but he was too weak to embark on a technique that he had never tried before. It seemed to me that the essential element was forgiveness. I knew my father was a believer and that he prayed every day to certain spiritual beings. I summoned them and imagined a white light all around us.

'Dad, we're going to pray together. I'll say a few phrases, and you can repeat them after me. If I make a mistake, tell me, and we'll put it right.'

He blinked. Slowly and carefully, I began to tell the story he had just told me, and he repeated each phrase after me, unburdening himself. Sometimes he even added phrases of his own, which was even better.

Then I began the second phase, of acceptance and forgiveness. I took my time so that he could assimilate the words fully.

'My parents did what they could, given the love they received and especially the love they didn't receive. I forgive them for having acted wrongly by me. I want to be at peace with them now.'

His eyes filled with tears.

'It's true,' he whispered, 'my parents did what they could, thinking it was for the best.'

Finally, I asked him if he wanted to ask forgiveness of anyone. He closed his eyes again. Despite his exhaustion, he managed to murmur a name. It was then, at the height of his distress, that my father seemed strongest. What courage it must have taken, at the age of seventy-seven, to open his heart in this way. I felt the immense strength of his love. Just as I was taking him in my arms to tell him how much I loved him, Stéphane came back into the room with my mother. 'I can't believe how much better you look!' she cried. It was true: a little colour had returned to his cheeks and he seemed calmer. A nurse came in and we left, feeling reassured.

My father was discharged from intensive care the next morning, and three days later he was transferred from the specialist cardiovascular unit to a normal hospital room. The nurses kept telling him that it would take at least a month to recover from such a severe case of pneumonia, but a fortnight later he drove himself and my mother back to their home, 230 kilometres away.

Thanks to my father, I witnessed the immense power of forgiveness. When he forgave, the cells of his body were reconnected to his embryonic memory – an exceptional source of growth energy – and life began to flow through him once again. I thank my father from the bottom of my heart for this lesson, one of the most important I have ever been taught. It was a powerful moment that was to prove transformative in my life.

Full of this new appreciation of forgiveness, I repeated the techniques in relation to anyone with whom I had been in conflict, and who had caused me suffering. As I asked for love or peace between us, I thought about the energy of forgiveness. I took time to feel it flowing through me and I cried with joy. I freed myself from vestiges of anger that I hadn't even been aware of, and immediately felt lighter.

- *Forgiveness isn't just a way of warding off bad karma – it's the ultimate healing tool, a renewing fluid that can reduce the impact of old ordeals and severe diseases.*

- *When we practise the techniques, our state of mind shifts. Our bitterness dissipates and forgiveness finds its way into us, a little further each day. When we repeat them, the message from soul to soul is communicated with a slightly different energy, and the benefits are greater.*

Take Time

I have witnessed the power of forgiveness on many other moving occasions, all of which showed me the importance of taking time. One day, a friend asked me if I could help one of her colleagues who had a severe **back** problem. He needed major spine surgery, which would leave him with an 80 per cent risk of being paralysed. Gabriel had been a sports coach before being immobilised by pain for over a year. According to my own research, a serious or paralysing illness requires us to scrutinise our lives, tend to our wounds, free ourselves from our secrets and, above all, forgive.

I began to work with Gabriel, and very soon I *sensed* his main wound. Given the urgency of the situation, I got straight to the point and suggested that he might have suffered in the past due to a betrayal by his father. 'It's unlikely. He disappeared and I haven't seen him for twenty years,' he said. I added, gently, 'You know, I've learned that brothers and sisters, just like twin brothers . . .' I didn't even have time to finish my sentence before he burst into tears. He explained that he had recently discovered that his father had a twin brother who had seduced his father's fiancée and eventually married her. A huge betrayal. His father had subsequently married another woman and had a child (Gabriel) with her, but had never played much of a role in this child's life: Gabriel in his turn had experienced this as a betrayal. Wanting to set him on the path towards emotional freedom, I pointed out that his father had been too overwhelmed by suffering to give his wife and son the attention they deserved. Gabriel agreed. Having been full of anger and hatred for so long, he was now filled with a sense of guilt at not having spoken to his father for twenty years. His current state of paralysis was allowing him (even forcing him) to stop and heal his wound of betrayal, and perhaps his father's, too.

I suggested how he might cleanse himself of this transgenerational burden and of his sense of guilt, stressing the fact that the ultimate aim of this process of liberation was forgiveness. Three months later, his health began to improve. The operation was successful, and he completed his self-exploration with a few sessions of EFT (short-term therapy aimed at coping with trauma). Three years later, he could walk normally and finally felt at peace.

When I think back to my double slipped discs, I remember that four years elapsed between my physical collapse and the day when I was able to begin the process of forgiveness. It seems a long time, but in the context of a lifetime it's very short. Be patient! It's worth the wait, but it's hard to stay motivated unless you're seeing gradual improvement. If you can't see any, it means you haven't identified the origin of the problem, or that there are other issues that need investigating. Ask yourself if your intention is really sincere. Perhaps your resentment and anger are too strong for you to progress. This may not be the right time: take a break and reread this chapter when you feel ready. Forgiveness is a slow process.

> *It's a good idea to ask your children for forgiveness: 'I know that my lack of tact, my anger and my suffering may have hurt you, and I ask you for forgiveness.' Forgiveness can be granted in the mind or out loud, depending on the situation.*

How Do We Know If We Have Forgiven?

We might sometimes be tempted to make assumptions about our feelings: 'Of course I've forgiven!' In order to ascertain whether or not we really have forgiven someone, we need to pay special attention to the way we talk about them. If we still feel the urge to call them names, then forgiveness is still clearly a long way off! But how do we know when we have actually achieved it? There's one clear sign: when we become aware of what we have gained from our own ordeals. Our suffering has helped us to develop. Are we capable of thanking the person who caused it? If we're not quite ready, it doesn't matter. Life is a long journey and things will feel different in the future. If we're at peace and the other person still takes an aggressive stance against us, not seeing that we have changed, we must accept that in the end this is their problem, not ours. We can't all advance at the same pace, so we must simply forgive and give thanks in our minds, rather than in person.

If forgiveness feels impossible at the moment, don't give up. The techniques will help you, as this example shows. One day I met a woman called Martine at one of my workshops. She was full of resentment against her mother. 'Why did she mistreat me, but not my brothers?' she kept asking herself. As I explained the idea of domination to her, she realised that her mother had been *feeding off* her daughter's energy. I asked Martine if her mother had experienced a trauma that could have left her *empty* or *dissociated*. 'She was raped,' Martine replied. I explained that ever since, her mother had been trying to fill this emptiness by *vampirising* her daughter, because Martine's energy was the energy she *preferred*. Surprised by this way of seeing things, Martine suddenly stopped characterising herself as the victim. She carried out the soul recovery (technique 6) and cut all ties of suffering (technique 8) with her mother, going through the whole process twice. After the second time, she wrote to me to say that the forgiveness that had seemed unimaginable not so long ago now felt possible, and that her mother's attitude no longer affected her.

Whom should we pardon first? We should begin with our parents, given that our souls chose them before being incarnated. There are many families in which one parent has abused a child, or caused trauma by violence, domination or spitefulness. The inner conflict provoked in the victim is sometimes too overwhelming to allow for forgiveness, let alone thanks. And yet, without forgiveness, we cannot reach the goal our soul is striving for in this life: recovering from our ordeals. We shouldn't blame ourselves – we'll get there in the end. As we distance ourselves from our sufferings, little by little, we will gain some perspective and progress towards our aim: the forgiveness of ourselves and others that will ensure our serenity.

- *All situations, even the most difficult to endure (war, murder, rape, disability, abandonment, divorce, death, harassment), are the manifestation of several wounds that our soul has chosen to replay. If we want to forgive, we need to understand that an ordeal is an opportunity to welcome the new person that we will soon become.*

- *We know we have forgiven someone when they cease to have any effect on us. Their actions become irrelevant and we can simply smile rather than getting angry. We know we have forgiven when we can THANK the other person for what they have done to us. We don't forgive for the sake of the other person, but for ourselves, for our soul, to end our suffering and, if need be, to heal.*

As we have seen, every ordeal is an opportunity for change, a path of learning, almost an alchemy. It was said that the philosopher's stone turned lead into gold: when we forgive, we turn our own heavy burdens into gold – a rebirth!

These introductory chapters are an invitation to a long interior journey. In the chapters that follow, the techniques work independently of one another. Drawing on the power of the invisible, conquering our fears, helping a friend, sharpening our intuition, cleansing our living space, facing bereavement and treating burns: thanks to the generosity of many mediums, hypnotists, geobiologists, shamans and therapists, I can show you how to do all these things, which will help us to live happier lives.

PART THREE

Your Emotional Health Check

Chapter 14

Never Alone Again

sn't it wonderful to be able to see the trials in our lives as necessary steps towards future rewards? Don't you find this philosophy comforting? The emotional cleansing that you have already accomplished has now reached the heart of your cells. You have rebuilt yourself and rediscovered your energy. There have been reconciliations, you have begun to forgive, and life feels easier: everything is possible. In order to fully establish this new way of perceiving the future, let's pursue more techniques designed to make our lives happier. The following methods form a sort of handbook for daily care, a way of increasing our serenity and happiness.

How to Find Your Guide

Let's begin with our 'guides'. We all have several guides by our side, and they can help us as long as we're willing to ask them. Unlike our *guardian angels*, we really do have to call on our guides if we want their help and, when we do, they manifest themselves in the form of a 'stroke of good luck'. They take different forms, but are always people who have passed away. They may be a family guide (a deceased family member), a spiritual guide (somebody linked to our career or passion) or a universal guide (somebody able to guide several people). We can give them different names:

'being of light', 'totem animal', 'source', or even 'the universe'. In China, they are known as 'celestial nobility'. Whatever we call our guide, they are our personal advisor, and we can talk to them out loud, as we would to a friend. Don't forget that if you don't call on them, your guide won't intervene. I became aware of my own invisible ally by way of my son, who was five at the time.

During my early life I felt, as many people do, that when it came to making big decisions in life I was on my own. By extension, if something good happened to me I took all the credit. I was wrong. One day, my son was playing in the living room. All of a sudden he began searching for a small object that he'd lost. He bent down to look under the sofa, found it, walked over to the window and said, 'Thank you,' looking up at the clouds. Then he sat down, and the moment passed. When I talked to him about what had happened, it became clear that *something* had helped him find whatever he'd lost. Who or what had it been? I asked him, and he pointed towards the sky and said, 'Them.' That was all. My Cartesian view of the world suddenly made no sense, and at the same time some memories from my own childhood came flooding back, from when my parents, sisters and I used to spend summers staying with my grandfather, who was a healer.

The front door of my grandparents' house had an opaque glass panel set into it, reinforced by wrought iron. From this door, a long corridor led to a mysterious room – the office – where nobody was allowed to go without the patriarch's permission. My grandparents were both hairdressers, but my grandfather devoted every afternoon to magnetism, an inherited gift that he'd been practising since he was eighteen. He was known as 'the healer', and people came to see him from all over France, hoping to be cured. Two walls of his office were covered with letters of thanks from those he had cured of all sorts of conditions: shingles, sprains, even infections. All the letters described the healing as wonderful and unexpected. 'I owe him my life' was a frequent comment.

My grandfather wore the same clothes, a suit and black tie, every day of the week. If my mother suspected that one of us was ill, he would pass his V-shaped divining rod back and forth in front of the child in question. If the ends of the hazel rod remained still, he would say, 'You're all right,' and the child was dismissed. One day, after waving his wand in front of me, he said: 'You've got a sore throat.' I nodded. 'Why didn't you tell your mother?' I murmured something about how it was all right, that the pain wasn't so very bad. I didn't want him to give me one of his home-made plasters, a sort of brown paste that he would heat up in a candle flame and drip onto a strip of cloth before fixing the cloth around my neck with piece of white tape. At home, when I had a sore throat, my mother would give me medicine or pastilles, and I preferred her method. I could almost have felt proud of wearing something 'magical', but I was worried that people might tease me. Still, although I used to complain, I had to admit that my sore throats cleared up much more quickly with the plaster than with medicine.

When he did his healing, my grandfather's hands were always hot. He used to say he had the 'fluid'. I remembered the boxes of peaches, nuts and tomatoes, the chickens and tins of pâté that he used to receive from patients who couldn't afford to pay him. I also recalled the innumerable times people from the village had told my parents that my grandfather had cured some ailment or other that doctors had failed to alleviate. These things were always confided in a whisper, with a hand resting on the other person's arm, and sometimes with tears in the eyes if the patient was a child.

I realised that the invisible, which had seemed normal to me until then, was something people didn't want to discuss openly. Rods, divination pendulums, magnetism: anything not easily explained by science was classed as 'bizarre'. Many people were suspicious of it, even afraid, but they often admitted that not everything could be explained by science, or that mystery had its place in our lives, just like love. Others didn't care about the whys and wherefores, as long as the outcome was positive. The local police often asked for my grandfather's help in finding people who'd gone missing, or who'd fallen into the river and drowned. He would ask for something that had belonged to the missing person – a toothbrush or a pullover – and then retire to his office to investigate with a detailed map of the area. He would mark the spot where the pendulum stopped, and the remains would always be found. He exercised his gift for fifty-seven years.

When he died, I became closer to my wonderful grandmother, and she became my priority. We had a lot of catching up to do. I no longer gave any thought to healing or unexplained phenomena. As though to distance myself from such things, the first articles I published at the beginning of my journalistic career were on the capacity of some plants to reduce pollution by absorbing formalde-hyde and trichloroethylene, climate change, and hormone disruptors. Then, all it took was a few enigmatic words from my son to remind me that I was the granddaughter of a healer. I began to read the books that had nourished his gift, and soon discovered the existence of guides, our invisible, infinite allies.

Let's learn how to make contact with them, and remember: a guide needs to be called on, so use it or lose it!

TECHNIQUE 10

Contacting your guide

1. You will need a white candle (white being the colour closest to light) and a match (it can only be used once, and, as this is a process involving intention, we don't want any other intention).

2. Say out loud: 'Dear guide, I'm happy to be making contact with you. Thank you for the help you will give me.' You can say exactly this or something similar, but it's important to remain spontaneous.

3. Light the candle.

4. Contact is now established. You can talk to your guide every day if you want to, and ask them anything you like. Warning: Asking for help doesn't solve everything. Please read the chapter below for guidance on how to proceed.

5. If you're trying to decide which therapist to consult, you can ask your new ally for guidance. Say out loud: 'Please, dear guide, [or please, universe] allow me to encounter the person who will help me to solve my problem [state the problem] this week.' It's important to specify a short space of time, so you can be sure that this person has been placed in your path by your guide. Speak with powerful intention.

6. When you leave the room, put out the candle and thank your guide.

If, during the next week, somebody mentions a therapist to you, go for it! It's a recommendation from your guide.

Ask the Impossible, But ...

You can ask your guide for help with anything: deciding who would be the best person to help you through the techniques, making a decision, finding the best person to carry out some work on your house, sending clients your way, giving you courage . . . You can ask them any time, and request that they show you the answer in a dream. Don't forget to thank them.

One day, on a long train journey, I got talking to an actor called Laurent. He was looking for an apartment after breaking up with his partner, but his precarious job situation meant that he kept being rejected by landlords. I explained how he could call on his guide, and he said he'd give it a try, using the term 'universe' because it was the one he felt most comfortable with. Here's the message he sent me three days later: 'Hi Natacha, just a quick message to let you know how things are going. I'd forgotten about the ritual until the day before yesterday, but I was still struggling to find anywhere to live so I gave it a try. An hour later, I got a call to say that a landlord had accepted me as their tenant. Unbelievable! I signed the lease and I'm moving in on the 30th. I wanted to share that with you.'

An hour later! Why would anyone not want to be guided in this way?

You can ask your guide anything you like, so don't hesitate to seek their help finding the right therapist to eliminate your symptoms or help you to explore your emotional past. To all those who might be tempted to ask me to recommend a therapist, I would say: 'Ask your guide!' Your body wants and needs this subtle connection, and the process is very personal. By asking your guide, you're likely to get a better result.

. . . What If Nothing Happens?

What action have you taken? If Laurent hadn't put so much energy into his search for an apartment, he wouldn't have been successful. 'God helps those who help themselves,' as the saying goes. If you are taking action and your intention is strong but you still see no progress, it might mean that:

- this isn't the right time for you;

- this isn't the right time for another person involved;

- the situation requires you to open your eyes to an emotional inheritance or an old wound, and can only improve when you have cleansed yourself of these things.

A failure is also a coded message from your guide.

Remember, I was unemployed and broke for four years before I was summoned for an interview by the employment agency, and discovered the masterclasses at the Luc Besson film school, but now I've been teaching there for four years. If I hadn't gone through the ordeal of being unemployed, I would never have had this opportunity.

It isn't vital to name your guides, but if you would like the reassurance of tangible, named presences the following technique will help you. I developed this ritual from a technique generously shared with me by the medium Maud Kristen.

TECHNIQUE 11

Finding the name of your guide

1. Stand in front of a bookshelf (at home or in a library).

2. Say out loud: 'Guide, please guide my thumbs to your name.' (If you don't say this, nothing will happen.)

3. Close your eyes (this is important!) and take a book at random.

4. With your eyes still closed, open the book and randomly place your thumbs on the pages, thinking about the guide you're about to discover.

5. Open your eyes and look under your left thumb, then under the right one. If your intention was clear, there will be a name underneath one of your thumbs. This is the name of your guide. If there is a name under both thumbs, your guide is either one of these or both. To make sure it's the good name, repeat stages 2, 3 and 4 repeating the words **'My guide, is your name . . .?'** Do it again with the other names. We don't look for a yes or no but for a sign such as a closed door as a no, or a smile as a yes. If there isn't a name under either thumb, read the left-hand page and then the right-hand page. The first name you read is that of your guide. If there are no names in the two pages chosen at random, look through the text to see if it brings to mind anybody from your deceased family. If an animal is mentioned, that is your 'totem animal'.

6. If the name isn't linked to anyone in your family, don't worry: this is the name of your **spiritual guide** or your **universal guide**. Only the **family guide** will have the same name as a family member.

There's no point repeating this technique several times. It would be like saying to your guide that you don't believe them. Finding your guide isn't a game, and we need to respect the sacred moment.

I once led a friend through this technique. He opened the book at a page where there were no names, so I asked him to describe the passage; it was the story of an old man who was travelling around the world by boat with his grandson. Suddenly emotional, my friend explained that his grandfather, who had since passed away, had taken him sailing when he was a child, and that this relationship had meant a lot to him. There was no doubt about it, he had found one of his guides. The therapist Stéphanie Crébassa also took part in one of my workshops and tried out this technique. The name revealed under her left thumb was 'Carl Gustav Jung', and under her right thumb was 'the forgotten name'. She asked me what this might mean. Her guide wasn't Jung, but did share one of his names, Carl or Gustav. But which? Luckily, the words 'the forgotten name' helped us: Carl is a more common name than Gustav, so Stéphanie's guide was called Gustav. She later found out from her mother that one of her ancestors had the same name.

If your thumbs reveal a full name, especially that of a well-known person, it doesn't mean that person is your guide. So if the name you see is Jack the Ripper, it doesn't mean your guide is the serial killer, just that their name is Jack. If the name is shared with somebody you know (a child or another family member), it doesn't mean that your guide is actually that person, just that they have the same name.

I described this technique on a programme called *Beyond*, and the episode has been watched online over 800,000 times.* Many people told me that they made contact with their guide after watching it.

Of all the examples I have given, Michèle's story is perhaps the most extraordinary. She closed her eyes, randomly picked out a medical book and opened it on a cross-section of the inner

---

* 'Se prémunir des vols d'énergie', *Beyond*, INREES.TV (INREES is the Institute for Research into Extraordinary Experiences).

ear. Underneath her thumb were the words 'Eustachian tube'. Eustache! A name. The most amazing thing was that her mother used to take her to the Saint-Eustache church in Paris, and always said that this saint would protect her. Michèle's mother knew instinctively that St Eustache was one of her daughter's guides. What were the chances of Michèle finding such a meaningful name in a medical book?

You now know the name of your guide and how to contact them. From now on, try to get into the habit of calling on them when you've got a difficult decision to make.

To end with, I'd like to tell a story told to me by Nicolas Lebettre, a former solicitor who became a therapist. He invited me to his home town to lead one of my workshops. That day, a friend of his was also there to help because Nicolas was very ill. The situation was critical: he was on the waiting list for a kidney transplant. At first I thought he wasn't paying much attention to the techniques I was describing, but he must have been interested by the method for finding a guide, because that evening he tried it out. He was astonished to realise that the two words under his thumbs made up the name of a now-deceased family member. It was a revelation. He allowed himself to believe in what had happened, and called on this guide for help. The next day, the hospital phoned to say they had found a compatible kidney for transplant!

The amazing thing about this technique is that it can help the most 'rational' thinkers to open themselves up to the invisible. Once you are in the habit of communicating with your guide, you will never be alone. Your guide is glad to help you, and talking to them is a happy, friendly experience.

3 METHODS FOR MAKING A DECISION WITH THE HELP OF YOUR GUIDE

1. Say: 'Guide, please help me to make a decision about this situation [give details].' Close your eyes, take a book at random, put your thumbs into it, still with your eyes closed, then read the lines under your thumbs. They are usually very revealing.

2. You can also call on your guide just before going to bed: 'Guide, please reply to this question [give details] and enlighten me in a dream.' Thank your guide in the morning, even if you can't remember your dream. If the answer isn't clear, repeat the process the following night – not forgetting to say thank you in the morning – until the response is clear.

3. Alternatively, you could write down the options open to you on slips of paper, fold them, mix them up, and ask: 'Dear guide, please draw my hand towards the right choice for [state your aims].' Say it with sincere intention.

   Take a piece of paper at random, read it, and don't forget to say thank you.

Chapter 15

Conquering Fears

D o you spend more time worrying about others than about yourself? For example, you're unemployed but spend most of your time looking after an ill friend rather than looking for a job; your relationship with your partner is faltering, but you put all your energy into helping someone else with their relationship problems; you're worried about someone you know suffering emotional abuse, not realising that you yourself experienced a similar ordeal as a child. It may seem nonsensical, but tending to other people's problems can be a way of closing our eyes to our own: the anxiety you experience on behalf of others hides your own fears. If you're obsessed with another person's problems but don't try to face your own, it may mean that:

- this person's situation has parallels with difficulties of your own, which you haven't faced up to;

- this person's situation reactivates an emotional wound that you haven't managed to identify;

- their problems allow you not to think about things that frighten you.

All this means that it is time to work on your fears.

Understanding Your Fears

Marie-Paule Jonathan, a transgenerational psychotherapist, explained to me that our fears take two forms: legitimate fears and irrational fears.

- **Legitimate fears:**

  These fears are linked to your personal circumstances. For example, you may fear running out of money, being criticised, dominating somebody, disappointing somebody or being unsuccessful. Or you may be worried about somebody you love being ill and not being able to help them. You may fear being abandoned, or having to live alone. These are 'small fears'.

- **Irrational fears:**

  These fears are created by our minds, and conceal legitimate fears. This is their reason for existing. They may relate to death (our own, our children's, our partner's, our parents'), or to losing our health or our reason. These fears have no specific basis (except if the person in question is ill, or if we have already lost a child). They don't result from intuition or premonition, because they are what we call 'screen' fears. These are 'big fears'.

Here's an example by way of explanation: if you're worried about running out of money, and at the same time your big fear is the death of a loved one, your big fear will generally dissipate when your financial problems are solved. When the 'little fear' disappears, so does the 'big fear'. Our minds have all sorts of subtle ways of camouflaging our fears, as this case shows: a young woman is frustrated by her father's stubbornness. He refuses to give up drinking and smoking, despite serious health problems. She finds this situation unbearable because she's afraid he will die early (her screen fear is her father dying). In fact, she's angry because this situation is making her relive a wound: she would like her father to listen to her, to get better, to thank her and to tell her he loves her. She's afraid his whole life will pass by without him ever having really paid attention to her. She also feels overlooked at work (her legitimate fear is that people will never truly value her). To solve her problem of recognition, she could remind herself that she *chose* this father for his faults and the difficult things he puts her through. Instead of trying to persuade him to change, she could cleanse the ties of suffering with him (technique 6 and 8) and seek the distance needed for forgiveness. Her father would be surprised to see his daughter growing more serene. Better still, he would be free of the incessant guilt of knowing that his daughter is expecting something of him, and would stop *punishing* himself by rejecting a healthier lifestyle.

We shouldn't wait until we're in trouble before working on our fears. It's up to us to identify them! Here are a few specific examples of how to go about this.

When Our Fear Relates to Our Children

Most parents worry about their children. We all want our children to be happy, and to avoid the kind of suffering we may have gone through ourselves. We want them to benefit from our experience, and the best method is to teach by example! But are we best placed to give advice about relationships if our own love life has reached a dead end? Can we really recommend a course of action if we're incapable of making decisions ourselves? Are we in a position to criticise a child who doesn't do what's best for them (work hard) if we are unable to do what's best for us (rest)? Is it possible to help our children if we can't perceive our own blockages? That's why it's important to work on our own problems first, and to acknowledge that our priorities for ourselves needn't be the same as our priorities for our children. Why shouldn't they have the right to make mistakes, to learn from life, and to acquire their own experience? Allowing a child to make mistakes gives them agency over their future, giving them the opportunity to recognise where they've gone wrong and avoid repeating the error.

If we think a child is 'dysfunctional', we also need to take a look at our own wounds, as this example shows: a mother once told me that her son had organised a party while she was away. Forty teenagers came, and left the house in a mess. She was furious and ended up shouting at him, telling him she'd never trust him again. Instead of apologising, he remained silent, which made her crosser than ever. But the real question remained: why had her son organised this party without telling her? She admitted that since she had split from her husband, her son seemed to be seeking attention from his friends by way of compensation. He was prepared to do anything to lessen his sense of abandonment. When she became aware of her own wound of abandonment, the mother realised that the scenario was repeating itself, so she worked on her relationship with her parents, using technique 9 relating to consolation. She immediately felt better, and came up with an idea to strengthen the bond with her son: she bought a packet of the sweets that he loved, and hid them here and there along his route to school. Then she sent him a text sending him on a treasure hunt: 'If you want to share some sweets with your friends, you'll find them on your way to school.' When he came home, he gave her a big hug and apologised. By identifying their shared wound (abandonment), she shifted her own interpretation of the situation and understood the motivation (wanting to impress his friends) behind her son's attitude.

We shouldn't talk to our children about our shared wounds. It's best to focus on ourselves, and that will have a positive impact on our children too. When they are grown up, they can choose to find out more about it if they want to, and we can discuss it with them then.

When Our Fears Affect the Health of Someone Close to Us

One of my friends has recently become a grandmother. At one point she became extremely anxious because her grandson kept regurgitating his milk. She and her daughter worried that he would become dehydrated, and took him to hospital. When I asked her about her past and her family, I learned that her grandmother had lost a daughter, and that she herself had spent her first few years in hospital seriously ill, as had her daughter. So three generations of mothers had feared losing their child! I suggested to my friend's daughter that she should talk gently but firmly to her baby, saying: 'You are regurgitating because you can sense my fears. These aren't your fears, they belong to me and to other women before me. I free you from these fears. Don't worry, everything will be all right now.' An hour later, she called me to say that her grandson had drunk without regurgitating for the first time, and they had left hospital.

Our children are mirrors. They assimilate our wounds and reflect them back at us. Every time you're worried about your child, look for the same problem in yourself. If your son is violent ... who behaved violently towards you? If your daughter has been abused ... who abused you when you were a child? Practise techniques 5 and 6 in relation to these people, but don't let your child take part. If your son is ill, which emotion do you associate with his symptoms? Practise techniques 6 and then 8, in relation to any members of your family who have experienced this same emotion. **Working on yourself is the best way to help your child.**

When Our Fears Affect the Love Life and Finances of Someone Close to Us

Nicole lives next door to a good friend of mine. One day, Nicole phoned me because she was convinced that somebody had practised black magic on her daughter. She explained that her daughter kept falling for men who abandoned her, that she had just sold her apartment for far less than it was worth, and that she had paid over the odds for a second-hand car. My instinct told me that the problems with men were a repetition of ordeals that her father had experienced. I asked Nicole if her ex-husband had gone through anything like this, and she told me he had never fully recovered from their divorce twenty years ago. I recommended that she show her daughter how to cleanse the ties of suffering with her father (techniques 6 and 8), making it clear that she loved him very much but that she no longer wanted to carry his difficulties. Then I asked Nicole about her own relationship with money, and she replied: 'I'm obsessed with it because I was poor for so long.' Nicole had transformed *her own fear of financial difficulties* into *fear that her daughter would have financial difficulties*. No black magic, just an unconscious projection of her fears. By working on these fears, she could ease her daughter's difficulties. Ideally, Nicole's daughter should also cleanse the ties of suffering with her mother by stating that this fear of financial difficulties doesn't belong to her, and that she no longer wants to carry it.

Don't forget that every ordeal is a blessing in disguise: an opportunity to heal our wounds, or those inherited from our family.

When Our Fears Damage Our Own Health

Noémie's mother is very manipulative, and her father died of cancer when he was young. Noémie thinks that he gave up on life as a result of his wife's tyrannical behaviour. When Noémie attended a routine breast examination not long ago, the doctor noticed several dark patches and booked her in for a biopsy. She then contacted me, and confided that she was afraid of dying young because of the ordeals that her mother had put her through. I recommended that she should practise the soul recovery techniques (5, then 6 in relation to her mother) and cut the ties of suffering (technique 8) with her, so that the manipulation could no longer continue. I also advised her to cleanse the ties with her father (technique 7) so that his soul could move towards the light. When the results of the biopsy came in, everything was normal and the dark patches had disappeared.

I once saw a message on Facebook from a therapist who was worried about a patient of hers who was due to have an operation. She called out to 'all benevolent souls to send positive energy to this young man'. That was a serious misjudgement, because she had no idea who would read the post. Somebody who has lost their own child may *unconsciously* resent another child for living, and thus send the wrong kind of energy. This also applies when somebody is suffering from cancer or another serious illness. I have sometimes seen calls on social media for 'everybody to use their energy, to help this person', but who knows which cells will receive this energy? The cancerous cells or the healing cells?

Achieving Serenity for the Sake of Our Family

- *We can't carry out this technique on behalf of someone else, because we don't have access to their soul. It should also never be carried out on children under eighteen (because their minds aren't ready, and they could suffer harm). We must never try to pressure someone into performing this exploration, because they may not be ready to face up to some of their past experiences.*

- *Nonetheless, we can ask our guide to communicate with the guide of someone we're worried about. If this is possible, the situation will improve.*

The brother of a friend of mine once went missing. He had been suffering from depression ever since his wife had left him, and he was also bringing up their two teenage children alone. He had recently begun a new job helping homeless people. One day he was meant to meet his sister for lunch, but hours passed and he didn't turn up. By the following day she had still heard nothing from him, but there had been no news of an accident and the police had made enquiries, to no avail. Extremely anxious by now, she phoned me. I suggested that we light a candle and make contact with his guide, who could then whisper to his soul: 'Whatever mistakes you have made, however exhausted and despairing you may feel, there is a solution. What you are doing for homeless people is wonderful, and you can feel proud of that. Keep going, we love you.' Her brother was found an hour later! His car had crashed on a winding road deep in the forest, which had made it very difficult to trace. Although seriously injured, he had eventually regained consciousness and managed to use his mobile to call for help. Given that his relationship with his daughter had recently become very difficult, and that he had been feeling unable to cope, this accident was undoubtedly a form of giving up. The message from his sister, which had passed from guide to guide and therefore from soul to soul, had allowed him to believe in life again. In other words, my friend saved her brother.

An ordeal is the universe's way of showing us that we are all connected. Every time we feel critical of someone close to us, or worried about them, we should have the humility to remember that they are mirroring us. To help those we love, we must first help ourselves. If we're finding someone's behaviour challenging, we should remind ourselves that we attract people and situations that highlight our own wounds. By freeing ourselves, we create serenity all around us.

TECHNIQUE 12

Identifying and eliminating fears

1. Do you always help others before yourself? This attitude masks your own fears (and an old wound).

2. Identify your irrational fears (death, physical illness, mental illness) and your legitimate fears (linked to your circumstances).

3. Address your 'big irrational fear' out loud: **'Until now you've been hiding my other fears, but I no longer need you to do that. I'm going to work on my old wounds and I don't want a veil drawn over them. You can go.'** Talk to it kindly, without anger.

4. Focus on your legitimate fears and try to identify which one is replaying itself. Ask your guide to advise you in dreams, or to guide you towards the right therapist to help you understand your blockages. Practise technique 7 or 8 to cleanse the ties of suffering if the recurring wound relates to a family member. Practise technique 9 if your wound is linked to a sense of guilt.

5. Talk out loud to your legitimate fears: **'Fear of . . .** [specify], **you can go now. I've understood that I keep reliving my wound of abandonment, injustice, betrayal** [etc.], **and I'm going to take steps to recover from it.'**

6. Visualise passing your fears up into the clouds, into the sea or into the wind.

7. Every day, note down three things that have brought you joy, pleasure or contentment. For example, you may simply have slept well, eaten a bowl of cherries or bumped into a friend. Help your mind to focus on what brings you joy. Sharing this ritual of happiness with another person helps us to cherish these moments, and is even more effective.

Chapter 16

The Power of Place

A Precious Ally

I n the West we tend to believe that 'where there's a will, there's a way', placing our desire at the centre of everything, but in the East this isn't the case. Marie-Pierre Dillenseger has been studying Chinese astrology techniques relating to energy for many years. She has often been called on by large companies as an expert on timing and spatial strategies, and is a respected teacher and communicator. She explained to me that in China, the success of an action is attributed to three factors: 20 per cent to our own activity, 30 per cent to the place where the decision was made and 50 per cent to the moment when we acted. In our own lives, many of us have probably observed that when it comes to our career, our family or our health, timing can have a big impact on our lives (something we experience as having a 'good year' or a 'bad year'). When we need to decide on something, Dillenseger recommends that we link our decision-making to the strength of our place (20% our home, 30% our work-place) in order to compensate for the vagaries of 50% of the time. In this way, we can avoid failing if the time is not right.

How can we draw on the strength of our place? As we all know, there are little shrines dedicated to 'spirits of place' all around the world. Florence Hubert, a former pharmacist and a medium with twenty years' experience, told me that there is a subtle energy present in all homes. Every place, whether new or old, has a guardian, a being all of its own. Of course, I could have dismissed this idea of 'spirit of place' as a nice superstition, a largely uninteresting psycho-magical protection, but the fact is that Florence Hubert's findings about physical places echo the beliefs of over 3 million people in China, India and Japan which are among the top 5 richest countries in the world. The psychotherapist Jacques Roques, co-founder of EMDR France (with David Servan-Schreiber), has this to say about the guardian of a particular place: 'We deprive ourselves of the psychic power of benevolent presences simply because they don't fit into predefined criteria, namely scientific ones.'

TECHNIQUE 13

Making contact with the guardian of a place

1. Position yourself in any room (energy is everywhere).

2. Address the guardian out loud: 'Dear guardian, I am happy to become aware of your existence and pleased to meet you. Today is the beginning of a collaboration.'

3. Greet the guardian whenever your thoughts turn to them, remaining cheerful, respectful and friendly.

4. If you ask the guardian for help, don't forget to give thanks.

The Guardian of a Place

In 2016, we were living in a rented apartment that had already been damaged six times by water leaking from the neighbours above. I saw an opportunity to try out this technique, and made contact with the guardian of the place: 'I'm delighted to make contact with you – please help us not to have any more leaks.' A year went by with no mishaps, but then Niagara struck for a seventh time, so I spoke to the guardian again: 'I don't understand why there's been another leak.' Before going to bed that night, I asked my guide to give me an explanation in my dreams. When I woke up, an idea suddenly occurred to me: the estate agent was obliged to ensure that the apartment was entirely habitable, but whenever there was a leak we had to wait for the room to dry and for an expert to sort out the insurance before repair work could even begin. Because of this, one room had remained unused for nearly forty-six months! I immediately calculated the reduction in rent that should have reflected the reduction in living space and, in the hope of obtaining some compensation that would help when we came to move house, I suggested that the estate agent should give us half of the actual sum. Naturally, my letter was ignored, so I handed over my calculations to a legal advisor . . . but also to the guardian, to whom I said: 'With this leak, you are helping us to obtain compensation that I hadn't expected. Please help us to receive this money, which will help us to move house. I leave it in your hands.' Two days before we were due to give notice, the estate agent sent us the money I'd requested. I couldn't believe it, and I immediately thanked the invisible ally in our home.

After that, I got into the habit of speaking to our guardian regularly. In the studio apartment in Paris where I used to do my writing, I would talk to the guardian and light a candle that I'd placed in a special candle holder. One day, I decided to sell the apartment. My prospective buyer was a young woman who worked in a bank and was sure she could arrange her mortgage loan before the end of the year in order to avoid extra solicitor's fees. By then it was autumn, and November and December passed with no news from her. In mid-January, she asked to visit the apartment again and I was worried that she might have changed her mind. The day after this second visit, the estate agent phoned me to apologise: as he'd been walking through the apartment, he'd broken the candle holder containing the candle I used for my communications with the guardian! I saw this as a sign, and immediately talked to this spirit of the place, telling it that I wasn't abandoning it, but simply wanted to go and live in the countryside where it was more peaceful. Then, I thanked it warmly for having helped me with my writing over all these years, and said goodbye. Five minutes later, as I was telling my husband what had happened, we were interrupted by a phone call from the solicitor, saying that the young woman had arranged her loan! Everything had suddenly fallen into place, after three months of waiting. It would have been very difficult to see this as simple chance. The guardian had been hoping for this final conversation, I'm sure of it. But could what had worked for me also work for other people? I still had my doubts, until the following scenarios finally convinced me.

At a workshop I led in January 2018, I suggested that those participants who had been manipulated by someone they knew might like to read my book *Les Blessures du silence* (*The Wounds of Silence*), in case it could help them. Isabelle did this, and she also explained to me that she wanted to leave her husband but that an ongoing legal wrangle with their neighbours was preventing her selling her house for eight years. There seemed no way out and Isabelle was desperate. Seeing no alternative, I suggested that she contact the guardian of her house and explain that she needed help to sell the house, and that it was a matter of survival. I stressed that she should thank the guardian for everything it had done, and make it clear that she absolutely had to leave. Six months later, she wrote to me: 'I spoke to the guardian of my house, and twenty-four hours later I got an email from our lawyer saying that there would be a decision about the legal dispute on 8 February, just two weeks later!' The verdict was given on 15 March, in Isabelle's favour. Anyone who has ever been involved in legal proceedings knows that the courts are overwhelmed with cases and the delays are usually interminable. Isabelle's case, which had been in limbo for eight years, was processed in seven weeks!

I once gave a lecture to former students of the HEC business school (now CEOs) in Paris in which I described the ways in which spirits of place can help us. I had assumed that these business leaders would have little interest in the workings of the invisible, but I was surprised by their keen interest. They asked me very seriously if there were guardians for yachts, and even the International Space Station! The answer is yes, as it is for every space! One of these CEOs told me that he used to talk to a big statue of a red dog in his office every day, and that it made him happy to think that this was the spirit of the place. Talking to a sculpture or an object is sometimes easier than talking to empty space, so why not take advantage of it?

One of my friends attended a workshop in which I discussed the subtle ways in which guides and guardians of places can help us. A month later, she called me: 'The first time I spoke out loud to my front door, I felt stupid. But before long, good things started to happen, so I set aside my Cartesian ideas and I now speak to my guide and my house guardian very regularly, as though I'd been doing it all my life. It has become completely normal to talk to my allies.'

This message, from Patrick, is even more moving. He is a doctor from Limoges, and after attending one of my workshops he wrote of his joy in actually *seeing* the spirit of the place where he was staying for a conference: 'I was blown away, because its kindness and warmth were immediately obvious. When I arrived in this town, I felt as though it had been expecting me!'

- The guardian is located just inside a house (or workplace), near the front door. It can be on the left or the right, depending on the space, but is also present in every room as soon as we call on it. We can ensure a good relationship with the guardian by making contact, talking to it, acting kindly towards it, greeting it, asking for its help in matters relating to the place, and thanking it. In a workplace, a large building or a group of buildings inhabited by the same family, there is just one guardian for the whole site. You can ask it to protect your space from hostile people.

- When you want to move house, ask for your guardian's support. Pack a few things into a box to prepare the way for your departure. Thank it for having welcomed you for all these years, then ask it to help you find another good place to live.

- The guardian is attached to the place (and it is there even in a new building) and, if you leave, it won't follow. Remember to say goodbye before you go.

- If you have a garden, it will have a guardian too, in the form of a tree. Ask it to keep a watchful eye on your house and look after everything in the garden.

Chapter 17

Protecting Yourself

Put Down Roots

When we've been living in a state of imbalance for years, how do we start to put things right? A first step, practised throughout the world, is to place ourselves back in a 'neutral gear'. This means anchoring ourselves and, more specifically, putting down roots. By visualising yourself as a tree, you will gain stability.

TECHNIQUE 14

Putting down roots

Use a Dictaphone or a smartphone to record – slowly – the following instructions.

1. Stand up, your feet parallel and slightly apart.

If you use a wheelchair, imagine that you are standing up (remember the incredible power of your mirror neurons).

2. Choose the tree with which you are going to create a link. It can be a tree in your garden, in a park or forest, or one that was familiar to you when you were a child. It needs to be straight, as trees with twisted trunks have been

subjected to disturbances coming up from the ground
and telluric forces, so it's best to avoid this kind of energy.

3. Close your eyes and imagine you are this tree. Your head
and arms are its branches. They are connected to the
sky. The sun warms the upper parts, and there is a light,
pleasant breeze. Your chest is the trunk of this tree,
standing straight and strong. It goes down through your
hips, legs and ankles. At your feet, two large roots push
powerfully down into the ground. These roots go
towards the centre of the earth, slowly drawing up
energy from under the humus. Each of these two roots
creates dozens of smaller ones, and hundreds of white
rootlets that absorb this energy. Your roots find water
and rich earth. They continue to grow, probing further
down, meeting layers of clay and sand, coiling past
stones and continuing their descent towards the centre
of the earth. Your two big roots and all the rootlets
gather the energy you need. They draw up the strength
and stability so generously offered by the earth. You go
down deep into it, towards the nurturing warmth.

4. Now, imagine coming back up along your roots. They are
filled with energy, trace elements, water, nourishment,
stability, strength and everything else you need. Come up
slowly along your roots . . . and your rootlets . . . and feel
the power they contain. Come up . . . carefully . . .
continue to climb with this positive energy and
essence . . . This stability is within you.

5. Finally, you reach your feet. Welcome the feeling.
Continue to follow the energy up through your calves,
your knees, your thighs and your hips. Store the energy

around your navel, your centre of gravity. You are now connected to the centre of the earth by your roots, and to the sky by your branches, in perfect alignment.

6. Open your eyes and thank the tree.

If you felt yourself *swaying* during this process, it means that you weren't anchored firmly enough. Repeat it tomorrow, and for a few days running, until you feel real stability. When we've been knocked about by difficult experiences, being rooted helps us to remain upright in the storm. And if we've been listening to a friend's troubles, or if we're a therapist, practising this rooting process allows us to put ourselves back into 'neutral'.

Christophe Noël, an energy therapist, wrote to me about this: 'I carry out *cleansing* on houses (when they have negative energy) and I occasionally also conduct exorcisms. Despite all the precautions I take before an intervention of this sort, I often find the process completely draining, and have to ask colleagues for help towards the end, when I can't complete it alone. I've noticed that since practising the rooting technique that you taught us, I haven't suffered from this in any of the three sites I've worked on, and I can tell you that one of them was full of particularly strong presences!'

Time for you to put down roots!

Cleanse Your Cells

We are now going to look at how, just as we shower and dress carefully in the mornings, we can cleanse our energy and the subtle information that surrounds our atoms. Some people call this our aura. The following technique is used when your energy envelope is polluted by fears, anger, anxiety, or sometimes guilt. This pollution interferes with your internal radar, your intuition, causing you to make mistakes in your daily life. I would like to thank Florence Hubert once again for sharing this technique.

TECHNIQUE 15

Cleansing your cells

1. You will need a bundle of dried white sage sticks (from a herbalist or health store). You will also need an empty glass and some matches.

2. Light the ends of the sage sticks and blow on them gently, just enough to extinguish the flame. The sage will now give off thick white smoke. Place the bundle of sticks in the glass and put it on the floor.

3. Stand above the glass with your feet slightly apart so the smoke rises up between your legs to your first chakra point. If you use a wheelchair, place the glass under it.

4. Read the following words aloud, taking the time to visualise what you are saying. Again, your intention is key here: 'I thank my guide and the archangels Gabriel, Michael and Raphael for helping me rebalance my cells.' Now breathe in and out deeply three times through your mouth, noticing how your stomach rises and falls. Then say: 'May everything ugly, dark or painful go away now, through the energy of the archangels. I thank my guide and the archangels Gabriel, Michael and Raphael for removing the obstacles in my energy. May my negative

thoughts, and the negative thoughts belonging to others, now move away into the light.'

5. Visualise the smoke from the sage sticks enveloping you. Continue: 'May everything that belongs to others, everything that holds me back, everything that is unfair, move away into the light. May everything that is displaced return to its proper place.'

6. Breathe in and out deeply again, three times through your mouth, allowing your stomach to rise and fall. Finally, say: 'May all the little positive energy cells return to their positions around me, may all my light return, and may all my chakras realign themselves, from top to bottom and bottom to top, regaining their colour and their position. May all the little positive energy cells circulate in their own rhythm and direction. I thank my guide, the beings of light, and the archangels for this rebalancing.'

7. Breathe deeply through your mouth again three times, allowing your stomach to rise and fall.

8. Repeat the whole process three times.

Don't forget to extinguish the sage sticks by tapping the end on a stone so the leaves don't burn away. That way, you can use them again next time.

Purify Yourself

I have perfected the following cleansing technique by integrating the most effective elements of a dozen or so purification rituals, with the help of medium and healer Loan Miège. She advises that anything harmful to us should be sent back to its original place. This technique doesn't require any objects, so can be practised easily by anybody.

TECHNIQUE 16

Purification

Say out loud: 'I thank my guides, the beings of light and all the higher benevolent spirits for helping me in this purification. Please take all my negative thoughts and all the negative thoughts belonging to others, and dissolve them in purifying light. Please take anything around me or within me that is holding me back, and send it back to its original place. Please take any unresolved conflict and painful memories, and bathe them in light so that they are healed in this life and in all the others. Please help my bodies of energy to reposition themselves perfectly, recentred around my physical body. May everything be balanced and harmonised. Please help the whole of my physical body, my body of energy, my aura and all my different planes to be totally cleansed, purified, balanced and harmonised. May the whole of my energy structure be repaired and balanced. Please bathe me in light, positive energy, and universal love. I thank my guides, the beings of light, and the higher benevolent spirits for accomplishing this purification and for their protection.'

If you are sometimes disturbed while you are practising these techniques, or if you want to reinforce your protection in your daily life, say: 'May an infinite light come into me and fill me with its strength!' That may be sufficient, but, if you feel you need further protection, visualise a translucent gold and purple bubble all around you, like a soap bubble passing under your feet and over your head, and say: 'May all the negative energies and thoughts belonging to other people move away from the bubble. Only my positive energies and thoughts may stay inside this bubble of light.'

After a long day at work, full of problems needing solving, we usually come home feeling tired. By practising one of these techniques, you will feel a real sense of freedom. Remember: all these rituals should be practised regularly, alongside your work on your fears and your emotional wounds.

Mediums and healers often say that 'water interrupts negative thoughts and actions'. This is particularly true of salt water. If you have the opportunity to visit the seaside, be sure to go for a swim and visualise a purifying effect on your ideas, thoughts, fears and guilt, and on any of these things that belong to others.

There is another method you can use alongside this one, in order to draw on natural resources to increase your strength.

Re-Energise Yourself

TECHNIQUE 17

Energy ritual with a tree

1. In a forest, a park, or your own garden, choose a tall, straight tree.

2. Stand a few metres away from it and (in your head rather than out loud) ask its permission to approach it. Let yourself be *sensed* by the tree, as you would with an animal.

3. Once the connection is established, move towards the tree and rest your head against its trunk, facing either towards it or away from it. Ask it to give you energy.

4. Imagine the sap entering your body via your feet, and bringing you strength, gentleness and benevolence.

5. When you begin to feel the benefit, you can thank the tree. This 'mental hug' can provoke strong emotions: vary the sensations by practising the technique with a young tree.

Trees have existed for 380 million years, whereas humans only came on the scene 6 million years ago, so trees are the grandparents of life on Earth. Let's spend as much time as we can with them, respecting them and allowing ourselves to be enriched by their presence. Reconnecting with nature is a wonderful way of rediscovering happiness.

Protect Yourself From Yourself

Why is it so important to free ourselves from our negative thoughts? Because they release information. When we express our thoughts out loud we give them extra energy, and, as our bodies are mostly made up of energy and information, everything we think and say is stored up in our cells.

If you feel hatred for somebody, your body absorbs this energy and you then carry it inside you. Strange as it may seem, you will feel a disturbance in your daily life, and a series of negative consequences is sure to follow. People close to you, or even strangers (in shops, on the road, clients, social media connections) will begin to act aggressively, seemingly without reason, in a reflection of the thoughts that you are unconsciously projecting. This could give rise to the following sequence of events, for example: 'This morning I argued with my boyfriend/girlfriend on the way to work. The driver in the car behind had a go at me because I didn't see the lights change, and to top it all off my colleague made fun of me when I came up with an idea.'

When you think negative thoughts about a person, or criticise them without trying to understand why they act the way they do, you are changing your own 'vibrational energy'; the frequency of your energy is modified. This makes you interpret events negatively because you are surrounded by the energy of the words you used to describe the other person. In other words, you see the glass as half empty and miss opportunities because your cells are not properly aligned. Your thoughts have an impact on everything you do.

The Korean Buddhist master, the Venerable Seongnam, showed me a very clear way of visualising the effects of our thoughts, actions and words. To represent the process, position your hand in the shape of a gun, with the index finger pointing forward, the thumb upwards, and the three other fingers folded towards you.

Your index finger represents your thoughts and actions; what you give or what you think. Your upward-pointing thumb is what the universe produces when it reinforces your thoughts and actions. And, finally, your three other fingers are what comes back to you, threefold. What we think and do is

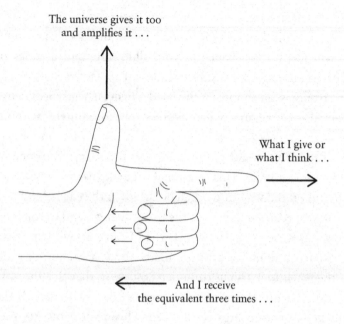

The universe gives it too
and amplifies it . . .

What I give or
what I think . . .

And I receive
the equivalent three times . . .

reinforced by the universe, and returns to us multiplied by three. If you criticise someone, several people will criticise you. If you steal from someone, you will lose a lot by another means. Similarly, if you act generously you will receive a lot in return.

In short, if you look on the positive side of things life will smile back at you in return. It's all related to the energy circulating around you and within you. The more you respect others, the more others respect you. If you are tolerant towards yourself (for example, if you say to yourself, 'I didn't get it exactly right, but I did my best'), you are likely to be more tolerant towards others, and others will be more tolerant towards you. You will be living better.

This image reinforces the idea that our wounds cause us to attract certain people and situations. You might benefit from asking yourself what your own thoughts have been focused on today . . . Your way of thinking can radically change your future.

Everyday Happiness

TECHNIQUE 18

Finding happiness

1. Say out loud: '**I wish happiness to** . . .' Say the words decisively, with all your heart.

2. Choose three people to whom you are going to wish success, good health and serenity. This is easy for people you're close to, but do the exercise for strangers, too. Better still, if you feel able, do it for somebody who annoys you or who has hurt you in some way. The important thing is to do it sincerely.

3. Observe how you are feeling. If you practise this benevolence every day, making sure to choose three different people each time, you will soon feel happier and find a smile returning to your face.

4. Stay positive, and the universe will amplify this energy circulating around you.

Several mothers who were worried that their children would fail an exam practised technique 18 before the exam, during it, and just as the results were coming out. They told me how surprised they were by their children's success. Achieving a state of serenity (rather than fear) is the best way we can help those around us.

Chapter 18

Sleeping Better

France has the highest consumption of sleeping pills and sedatives of any country in the world. Dr Patrick Lemoine, a psychiatrist and sleep specialist whom I interviewed about this, explained how worrying the situation is: 'The Health Ministry advises that medication shouldn't be the first port of call, and that relaxation techniques or cognitive and behavioural therapy should be tried first, but it only provides funding for medication. This creates a real problem, because studies have shown that of 100,000 patients treated, the risk of death doubles among those who take benzodiazepine for more than three months, and they can also suffer memory loss, and are at increased risk of dementia and Alzheimer's. If treatment is stopped too suddenly, it can cause epilepsy and serious disorientation.'*

The quality of our sleep can be a cause of anxiety. If you are over sixty-five and worried that you no longer sleep like a baby, you may be reassured to know that Lemoine says that, with age, sleep becomes lighter, and we tend to wake more often in the night. This is normal, and there is no need to take sedatives or sleeping pills to 'repair' what is actually your new natural sleep

---

* Dr Patrick Lemoine, *Dormez! Le programme complet pour en finir avec l'insomnie* (Hachette, 2018)

cycle. Accept that your night will include periods of wakefulness, and that this is in the natural order of things.

It's All About Waking Up

How can we tell if we've had a good night's sleep? Lemoine tells us that if we feel full of energy when we wake up, have no trouble concentrating, and don't suffer from any kind of memory loss during the day, it means all's well. 'It isn't actually sleep that matters, it's how we feel when we wake up,' he says. But if you wake up feeling tired, how can you improve your sleep?

ADVICE FOR SLEEPING BETTER

1. If you take sedatives, ask your doctor to reduce your dose gradually.

2. Take plant extracts such as valerian, passion flower or camomile, in the form of herbal teas or tablets. You can also ask to be prescribed melatonin (a naturally occurring hormone that signals to your brain that it is time to sleep).

3. Take a course of therapy designed to reduce stress, such as sophrology, acupuncture, hypnosis or EFT.

4. In the evening, set aside a period of time between arriving home from work and going to bed. Choose a calming activity such as reading, knitting or watching a film on television: it's important to have pre-sleep rituals to allow your body to learn them and respond to them. Work with your body.

5. Avoid tablet or smartphone screens that give out blue or white light; these colours reduce melatonin production and thus prevent and disrupt sleep.

6. Take a lukewarm bath or shower before bed: reducing your body temperature encourages sleep. In the morning, on the other hand, wash in hot water (because raising the body temperature stimulates the production of hormones associated with activity).

7. Make sure there are no objects giving off electromagnetic waves near your head: electric alarm clocks, lamps, mobile phones, cordless phones, internet routers, etc.

8. Avoid sleeping on a mattress with springs, as these can also increase electromagnetic activity.

9. Sometimes, underground energy sources cross and generate harmful waves, known as negative telluric points. Sleeping above one of these may disturb your sleep, so try moving your bed slightly, or sleeping in a different room, and compare your sleep quality. You may even observe an improvement in your health. If in doubt, consult a geobiologist.

10. To help you sleep soundly, don't have a television in your bedroom and don't work in bed: keep your bed for sleep. Finally, remove your 'emotional dustbin' from your bed (see technique 19).

Avoid Overloading Your Body

Sometimes we fall asleep quickly but then wake up in the middle of the night and can't drop off again. The doctor and acupuncturist Robert Corvisier explains this phenomenon through Chinese medicine. We may experience anger a few times over the course of the day, and it is the liver that *digests* this emotion during the night, as well as breaking down the complex molecules found in sugar, alcohol and fat. Despite being the largest organ in the body, the liver can't always cope, and when it becomes overloaded it passes some of the burden on to the spleen, which tends to do most of its work at around four o'clock in the morning. This explains why we often wake up around that time: it's a message from our body saying that our liver is overloaded. When this happens, you may want to consult a therapist with expertise in detoxifying the liver and the spleen (using shiatsu, acupuncture, psycho bio acupressure, etc.).

Cleansing Your Home's Energy

It's better to cleanse our beds first because we tend to bring all our worries to them: we work in bed, write emails, watch sad or scary films, and discuss the frustration and anger we may be feeling towards our family and friends. The place where we sleep therefore tends to be polluted by our emotional turmoil, and we may find that, even if everything is going well in our lives, our more negative thoughts tend to gain the upper hand once we're in bed. This is because when we're at rest, we give ourselves up completely to our unconscious minds and to the energies around us.

This cleansing technique was generously shared with me by the geobiologist Vincent Navizet, whose practice uses tools (Lecher antennae, divination pendulums, rods, etc.) to examine the waves emitted through crevices or irregularities in the earth's surface.

TECHNIQUE 19

Cleansing your bed's energy

1. Stand on one side of your bed, your arms stretched out sideways and your palms facing upwards.

2. Say out loud: 'May all the negative energy and thoughts in this place disappear into the earth.' Breathe deeply and lower your arms towards the ground as though you are guiding this energy down into the earth.

3. Then: 'If any negative energies remain, may they be taken into the light by the archangels Gabriel, Michael and Raphael.' Lift your arms to the sky as you say these words. (If you feel uncomfortable calling on the archangels, say: 'If any negative energy remains may it be taken into the light.')

4. End by saying: 'May the space be filled with love and light.' Then give thanks.

If you live in an apartment, or your bedroom is above another bedroom, don't worry: you haven't sent the energy pollution into your neighbour's bed! It has gone straight down into the earth and been dissolved.

Carry out this process for all the rooms in your house. Once a month is enough, but if you argue with your partner, or wake up feeling tired after a difficult night, repeat the ritual straight away. You can also do it in a hotel or if you are staying with friends. Similarly, you can carry out this process in all the rooms of your house, thanking the guardian of the place for helping you with the cleansing. And, as with all techniques involving a request for help, don't forget to do it with strong intention and a smile on your face.

Chapter 19

Cultivate Your Intuition

We boast that we are far more intelligent than animals, and yet when it comes to making decisions a multitude of emotions intervene and we are assailed by doubt, wavering like seaweed in the ocean, whereas animals act quickly and shrewdly, through instinct. How can we learn to make the right choice? How do we make decisions?

Listening to Your Body

I became aware of my own intuition through contact with the natural world. I was making a series called *Les Héros de la nature (Heroes of Nature)* for the France 5 television channel, focusing on the work of people who were fighting to save threatened animal species. I crossed the world, travelling on an ice-breaker in the North Sea with whales nearby, navigating the Amazon in search of bats, having a brush with death in Borneo to help orangutans, and crying with joy encountering elephants in Uganda. One day my cameraman and I were filming a group of hippopotamuses by a lake when, instinctively, I said: 'That mother is going to get up and walk behind that bush with her baby.' And she did exactly that a few seconds later. We were amazed! The same thing happened with cheetahs, crocodiles, even platypuses. I realised that I had managed to connect with the animal world.

Some time later, my husband and I went travelling in order to produce an article for *Géo* magazine documenting our experience of shamanic initiation. He was taking the photographs and I was writing the text. During the course of this experience, we learned that it is possible to communicate with what the shamans call 'teaching plants', and I realised that my connection with nature also extended to plants. The strangest thing was that this intuition began to manifest itself almost without my knowing it, in my everyday life.

Thanks to an observation made by the producer Thierry Berrod, I realised that the subjects I took an interest in often became the focus of big news stories a few months later. For example, one day I read a scientific article by the German researcher Hans-Hinrich Kaatz in which he demonstrated that some genes from genetically modified rapeseed plants had been transferred to bees by bacteria. An image of these insects dying in huge numbers immediately formed in my mind. I decided to write a futurist novel based on this idea, and I contacted Swiss, German, American and French researchers to learn more. Eleven months later, the first mass death of bees made the headlines. Thanks to all my research, I was able to produce the first French film on the subject, and was invited by the French National Centre for Scientific Research (CNRS) and the Natural History Museum to take part in a conference about it.

I have been struck by similar intuitions on several other occasions. I once made a documentary about autism, and five months later the condition became a national talking point. Similarly, I wrote an article sounding the alarm about the first case of blue-tongue virus in sheep in Germany. Eight months later, 31,000 European farms were affected. I developed an interest in ways of escaping harassment when I was writing my novel *Les Blessures du silence*, and, three months after I delivered the manuscript to my publisher, the Weinstein scandal broke. In 2016 I highlighted the potentially deadly consequences of a paracetamol overdose in another novel, *Les Racines du sang* (*The Roots of Blood*), and in July 2019 the French medicines watchdog recommended that a warning about the dangers of overdose should appear on all products containing paracetamol.

As I connected with things *greater than myself*, I developed my intuition. If I eliminate anything linked to my mind, with all its shifting fears and fantasies, the only remaining link between these experiences is my body. Our bodies *talk* to us all day, causing us to shiver, making our stomachs rumble, and tensing our muscles. They tell us when we are hungry, thirsty, tired, attracted or repulsed, and let us know if we *get* a person or don't *get* them, even if it's the first time we've met them. Thanks to my body, I have connected myself to the universal element that links us all to one another.

Your Inner Voice

This simple technique will help you to learn how to listen to the little inner voice that wants to help you. It must be carried out quickly so that your brain doesn't have time to interfere!

TECHNIQUE 20

Developing your intuition

1. Sit down, relax, and stretch out your legs.

2. Think about a situation in which you need to choose
   between two alternatives, and state them. For example:
   'I buy a bike/I wait to receive one as a present,' 'I order
   this pretty dress today/I wait until it's on sale,' 'I go to
   the cinema with X/I go with Y,' 'I get a loan from the
   bank/I ask such-and-such for a loan,' 'I tell my boss
   something/I don't tell my boss something.'

3. Close your eyes and call the first option to mind.
   Without thinking, observe what is happening inside your
   body **in physical terms**. Is your jaw clenching, are your
   feet curling up, is your chest slumping, is your pulse
   quickening? Or, on the other hand, are you relaxed, with
   no tension in your body? Is your heartbeat regular?

4. Once you have 'scanned' your body (ten or fifteen
   seconds is enough), call the second option to mind. Still

without thinking, observe what is going on in your body.
Focus on your sensations.

5. Compare the two sensations. Which was more pleasant?
   Remember not to ask yourself: 'Did I feel happy or sad?' or
   'Did I see a light?' because the answer to those questions
   will come from your mind. You need to go through the
   process quickly and remain a 'spectator' to your physical
   sensations.

The first time you do this, you may find the sensations so subtle that you're not sure what you're feeling. Even if there is only a very small difference, have faith in yourself! As you get more experienced, it will be clearer. Remember that our perception of sensations is personal: a tingling could be pleasant for some and unpleasant for others.

The more you practise this ritual, the clearer your perceptions will become. I sometimes even do this on the train when I'm trying to make a decision: I close my eyes and call the first option to mind for ten seconds, then the second. I'm used to listening to my body and I know how it expresses itself: my shoulders show me which way to go by curving or straightening. When you're up against it, trust your body. It's your best ally.

Feel free to note down your sensations to help you learn to recognise them. For some people, a 'yes' will be communicated by a tingling in the arm, and for others a 'no' will be signalled by a tense jaw or increased heart rate. If you feel nothing, or can't sense a difference between the two options, it might mean that:

- there is a third option you haven't thought of;

- neither of the options is feasible;

- it's difficult to distinguish between them. Asking your body is a new technique and you need more practice.

Sometimes the outcome may surprise us! During one of my workshops, I asked everyone to try out this exercise. Everybody came up with two choices and some agreed to share the results with me afterwards. One participant, a mother, told us that in answer to the question 'Should I allow my seventeen-year-old daughter to go out on Saturday?' her mind said 'no' but her body responded *physically* with a clear 'yes'. Saturday came, and her daughter went to the party; but, at eleven o'clock at night, her mother felt her body tense for no reason. Immediately worried, she tried to call her daughter, but there was no answer. She jumped in her car, and arrived at the house where the party was being held to find her daughter almost unconscious, being carried by two friends; she had ingested something harmful, but nobody knew what. The girl was immediately taken to hospital to have her stomach pumped, and soon recovered. The most important part is what the mother told me later. Seventeen years ago, she almost died while giving birth to her daughter, but the presence of the newborn baby had helped bring her back to life. The problem was that the girl subsequently felt that her mother owed her everything. 'Ever since I "saved" her, we've returned to our normal mother and daughter roles. For a month now, our relationship has been great and I owe it to my body!' It turns out that mother and daughter both needed this ordeal to rebalance their relationship.

- *Even if the answer given by your sensations seems strange, have faith in your body.*

- *Your little inner voice is actually that of your guide. By allowing yourself to connect with the subtlety within you, you are opening yourself up to links with other people, and much more besides.*

Chapter 20

Healing Burns

M any people's family trees reveal a great-aunt or a grand-mother who used to treat burns. The method tended to be passed on by healers on their deathbed, a secret communicated to the most sensitive child. Today, I think it's time to share these techniques more widely. It can save lives, so why should some people benefit and not others? Especially as it doesn't require a special gift. True, we won't all be capable of healing third-degree burns, but minimising the effects of a superficial burn on ourselves or others is something we can all do. And the more we do it the better we get! The main thing is to free ourselves of doubt.

In ancient times, people used to talk of *fire talkers* or *fire charmers*. Now, I think of my friend, René Blanc, a former firefighter from Thonon-les-Bains, near Lake Geneva. After his retirement, he continued to fight fire . . . in the form of **burns**. He would also heal skin problems caused by shingles or eczema. More often, though, he helped relieve the pain of burns caused by radiotherapy during cancer treatment. The oncology unit at the hospital in Lausanne often recommended his services to patients. He was very much in demand, receiving about forty requests for help every day. He only worked over the phone, and would sit at home, the receiver to his ear, and recite a prayer. The patient's pain would be immediately relieved.

Several studies have been carried out to try to understand the processes at work here, but no scientific explanation has yet been found. It isn't a psychological phenomenon or a placebo effect, because badly burned babies have been seen to stop crying straight after an intervention by a fire talker. The technique has also been shown to be effective on animals, who have no idea that somebody is trying to heal them. And we can't put it down to a transferral of energy, because the treatment is immediately effective even if the patient and the fire talker are 5,000 miles apart.

David Servan-Schreiber, a doctor and neuropsychiatrist who appeared in one of our films, says this: 'I've known cancer patients whose radiographer has said to them: "Given that the side effects are severe, especially the skin burns, I think you should consult a fire talker." That raises a lot of questions, because fire talking has no known scientific or rational basis. Nobody knows how these slightly magical incantations, often recited in Latin, prevent the skin being burned by something as aggressive as radiotherapy. What fascinates me the most is the understanding we have with a doctor: if you consult me, what do you expect of me? You expect me to recommend something I have every reason to think will benefit you, and every reason to think will not harm you. Nowhere in this contract is it stipulated that I must know how the treatment works, but I must be sure that it will do you more good than harm. So a radiotherapist recommending fire talking has understood this. If fire talking generally works for patients, and has no side effects or ensuing problems, it's the best possible medicine. And it's the most rational medicine. I don't know if it's scientific, but it's certainly the most rational, intelligent and logical, and that's what we all expect from our doctors.'

Many health professionals have taken the time to compare the outcomes of conventional techniques and fire talking, and have all come to the same conclusion: the burns *treated* by a fire talker heal better than those treated medically. We shouldn't underestimate the importance of this.

You can learn to be a fire talker too, by following the technique passed down by my grandfather, Raoul, who was a healer and fire talker. He shared the following ritual with me, and I am very grateful to him. And remember, as with the other techniques, the power of your intention is very important.

TECHNIQUE 21

Putting out the fire

1. You can murmur these words, or say them out loud if you wish: 'At the fountain of St Matthew, there were three bandits who wanted to burn the good Lord. St Matthew said to them, "Don't burn the good Lord, burn me instead." He placed himself at the mouth of the oven and the fire went out.'

2. Blow cold air onto the burn (with your lips pursed, otherwise the air will be hot), moving your head so that your breath draws the shape of a cross on the skin. If you are healing remotely rather than in person, blow out cold air and use your intention to focus on the patient's burn.

3. Repeat the whole process (words and breathing) three times.

Pierre Yonas, another healer, was kind enough to share his technique with me, for which I am very grateful. Again, this must be recited with a sense of confidence that the process will work, with faith in yourself: 'Fire, I will put an end to you. You have no place in the body of [give name]. Evil is expelled and good takes root.'

When the time comes for you to practise fire talking on somebody, choose the technique that *speaks* to you. It will work – you'll see. I have received an enormous amount of feedback telling me how effective it is. One day I shared my grandfather's technique during an interview for INREES, and soon afterwards I received this message from Emmanuelle: 'I would like to thank you and your grandfather for this precious gift. I was burned by a barbecue and tried out this prayer to relieve the pain. The burning sensation disappeared immediately and there was no blistering!'

A few weeks later, a mother wrote to me to say that she had *removed* the fire from her nine-year-old son using this ritual. I also received a message from a man who had practised it on his dog, which was suffering from eczema-related alopecia, and the dog had immediately stopped scratching. Now, after every talk I give, several people tell me they have extinguished the fire in various kinds of burns using this technique. I am always overjoyed to learn that they have been successful – as I thought they would be – even though the formula was not passed down from an ancestor.

Chapter 21

Staying Alive

Death is the big question, the greatest mystery of our lives. And when we lose someone we love, we are devastated. I'm often asked: 'How can we even begin to conceive of a benevolent universe when we lose a child, a parent or a spouse?' It seems inconceivable, of course. Is there any way of finding serenity when death has cast a shadow over us?

Grieving

When a loved one dies, we unconsciously begin the grieving process. I interviewed the psychiatrist Christophe Fauré, a psychiatrist who specialises in grief, who divides the process into four stages:

1. **Shock:** We don't fully realise what is happening to us because it is too violent and painful. We *anaesthetise* our own emotions. During this phase, we may manage to achieve certain things mechanically without even crying (such as organising a loved one's funeral without shedding a tear . . . before collapsing later on). This period may last a few hours or several days.

2. **Desperate search for a connection**: We try to connect with the person we have lost, through smells (their perfume, a toy that we refuse to wash), objects or clothes. We look at photographs of them, perhaps keeping one with us all the time, and we listen to our voicemails in order to hear them speak. This phase can last between eight and ten months.

3. **The destructuring phase**: During this period, we come to understand that our loss is irreversible. We miss the loved one more and more, and we panic because we feel that we're getting worse and worse as time goes on. In fact, this phase is normal and necessary, showing that we are progressing through our grieving process. This period is the hardest of all because it is the longest (sometimes going on for several years), and can make us feel that this is the way our life will always be from now on. However, the process is slowly moving towards the fourth stage.

4. **Easing**: This phase is to do with our connection with the person who has died. We allow ourselves not to think about them every day. We *sense* that they are within us, as a gentle and timeless presence. We feel less resentment towards others for not understanding what we are going through. Little by little, we begin to reintegrate into the world, and take on new projects. A sort of interior peace is established inside us, even though we feel irrevocably changed, and know that *nothing will be as it was before*. Some things have been taken away (our carefree state of mind), but other things – positive things that we might never have imagined – have appeared: insight into ourselves, into others, and sometimes into our whole approach to life.

It is only when we reach this last stage that we are able to view the death of this beloved person differently. Mediums tell us that a child or adult who dies before their parents do is a soul that has chosen to pass on in order to allow those around it to progress in a different way . . . sometimes over the course of several generations. The death is thus not our fault, or anybody else's fault, still less a result of bad karma or bad luck. By thinking of this terrible loss as something that our loved one has done for us, to allow us to see the future in a different way, we are paying homage to their soul. The best gift we can give them in return is to ask ourselves: how can I change, in order to move forward in life? What can I do that would make them happy? Which aspects of my thinking should I develop and nurture?

Life After Death?

Some believe that there is a life that continues after death, and that there is something 'on the other side'. For others, this is completely inconceivable. Interestingly, all those who have studied the question have found that their beliefs are challenged when it comes to the question of the survival of consciousness. There are so many accounts of deceased people sending a sign to their loved ones, or of a medium relaying information about things that have occurred after a death, that these phenomena cannot be covered by one simple belief system. My husband, the journalist and former war correspondent Stéphane Allix, engaged with these issues in his book, *The Test*, an investigative work for which he asked six mediums to contact his dead father.* He asked them to describe

* Helios Press, 2018.

the four objects that he had secretly hidden in his father's coffin, and even the most sceptical observers had to admit that the results were astonishing.

The cardiologist Pim van Lommel wrote about near-death experiences (NDE) in the scientific journal *The Lancet*: 'We should consider the possibility that death, like birth, allows us to pass from one state of consciousness into another.' The body is the receptacle for our consciousness, which continues its journey after death. Our deceased loved one exists somewhere else, without their physical form.

If we can manage not to lament the death of our loved one, and not to resent them for having abandoned us, we are helping them to evolve into their next stage. We need to accept that it was their *time*. In fact, many people sense that they are going to die before the moment actually arrives. My sister told my mother about experiencing a premonition that she would die young. Thomas, Stéphane's brother, told us when we were together in Afghanistan that he was looking forward to reaching the age of thirty because he was finally going to start *living*. We often don't understand the full significance of these hints until after the fact. Several months before his death, Stéphane's father said he wouldn't live to see the next Christmas, even though he wasn't yet ill at that point. A child we knew, the son of a friend, drew a picture of himself a few days before he died, clearly showing him with the red Lego brick that he was to swallow by accident a few days later, and which would cause his death. In other words, our soul *knows*.

Understanding the meaning of death, the greatest ordeal of all, is not easy. There may come a time, though, when things become clear, and we may even find that being confronted with death is a transformative experience. It was when my sister died that I realised my own urgent need to assess my life. It took losing her for me to find the strength to forgive. I spread my wings, and I owe that transformation to her. How many people have made radical changes in their lives following a bereavement?

My mother was seventy-four when her daughter passed away. They had always been extremely close, and she was devastated. She went through the four stages described by Christophe Fauré, finding the third phase, during which we feel as though we're getting worse, particularly hard. Then one day she allowed herself to begin working again, but in a different way. She began training social workers in mediation, using stories and puppets, and was surprised to discover that her approach was therapeutic for those she was teaching. They were able to free themselves and, with the help of a few props, to rid themselves of inner conflict. They didn't know anything about her bereavement, but they could see in her eyes that her soul had been through a process of rebuilding. She now emanated a sense of hope that we can recover from even the hardest blow. She is now eighty, and still working. Her students love her. She and my father have retained their sense of curiosity, and they travel all around France by car, visiting architectural and natural wonders. What strength, what power of reconstruction!

Seeking the hidden meaning in death is a homage to our loved one, the best way of ensuring that they did not leave us in vain.

If, when you count up the number of people you have lost, you feel that the total is unfairly high, think about this image: two people go to the market in their village, an athlete and a little boy. They buy their food and put it in a heavy basket, but who will carry it? The athlete, of course. We give the burden to the person best placed to bear it. This story shows that we have the strength to endure these ordeals, to recover and to heal.

Nevertheless, if you feel overwhelmed by your emotions, you

need to seek help. Don't hesitate to ask your guide, saying: 'I'm going through something very difficult. Please give me the strength to move forward and understand the meaning of this death.'

I no longer have any doubts about the survival of the soul. Those we have lost hear our thoughts and feel our emotions when we think of them. Let's carry out one last ritual to convince ourselves.

TECHNIQUE 22

Reconnecting with a deceased loved one

1. Think hard about the person.

2. Tell them out loud that you love them.

3. Focus your attention on your heart. A sense of plenitude and joy washes over you. Your loved one is at your side to comfort you. This contact is a subtle reconnection.

The day will come when the loss of this person ceases to make us cry. We realise that they are near us every moment of our lives, as soon as we think of them. They are living in our hearts for eternity.

Chapter 22

Upgrade Your Life

Living Your True Nature

Watching a lizard shed its skin is a revelation. It does it slowly, in stages, and when it's free of its old skin it walks more energetically, testing its strength. Thinking about this process helped me to realise that I needed to leave behind my old body and absorb all the changes in energy that had taken place in my soul and my mind. I had to separate myself from this too-tight skin that had known fear, sadness and anger. But how? Like the lizard, I decided to walk. What more fitting symbol than a walk to end this journey towards healing? I soon chose my route: Bordeaux to Lourdes on foot. It would be a homage to my grandmother, who used to make the same pilgrimage every year by train. I would walk the 309 kilometres alone, over two weeks, stopping in hostels along the way. I chose to do it in September, when the weather would be mild: the south-west is known for its Indian summers and the glow of the autumn sun. To get myself in shape, I walked every day for a month.

The first day of my adventure: after walking for twenty-one kilometres in the pouring rain I arrived at the guest house, and the sun finally made an appearance. Adele, the owners' five-year-old daughter, asked if I'd like to go and pick figs with her. They were wonderful. Her mother told me that the closest restaurant was three kilometres away, but, seeing the horror in my eyes (at the thought of putting my soaking shoes back on), she kindly offered to lend me her car. I couldn't believe my luck.

The next day I chatted to the housekeeper, Marie-José, about my interest in the invisible. 'I'm the same,' she said. 'Actually, my husband's a clairvoyant. He can see the dead, and hear them.' She added that when he was five, her son Raphael used to shout out in the night because he could *see* a man in the corner of his bedroom. When he was visiting his grandmother one day, he recognised the face of this *shadow* in a photograph album: it was a great-uncle who had died a long time ago and whose name was . . . Raphael. The boy's father explained that this ancestor was coming to thank little Raphael for carrying his name, and to protect him. The child stopped being afraid. Then Marie-José told me another incredible story. As Raphael got older, he began to play football, always in goal. One day, when he was fifteen, the team was playing against a team from Barcelona, and they needed to win the match in order to be promoted to a higher league. The match was a draw, so it came to a penalty shootout. Everything now rested on Raphael's shoulders. Suddenly he heard a voice: 'Up high, on the left.' He jumped in that direction and stopped the ball. He thought it was his father calling to him, until he realised that his father was sitting miles away in the terraces! The tips continued: 'Down low, on the right.' Raphael realised that it was his deceased uncle talking, so he followed *old* Raphael's instructions to the letter and won the match! The great-uncle was the boy's guide and, after that, whenever he asked for support in difficult situations, help was always at hand.

After two more days of walking in the rain, I arrived in Bazas. I got talking to the charming couple I was staying with, and the husband told me that their two-and-a-half-year-old daughter Eleanor was constantly pointing to *presences* that they couldn't see. I told them the story about Raphael and the football match, and they looked at me in surprise. They themselves had been living in Barcelona exactly a year ago! The strangest part was that at that time, their daughter never used to smile except when she went into her bedroom and looked into one particular corner. When they talked to her about this, they worked out that she was seeing her dead grandmother, whose name was also . . . Eleanor.

This journey became a chance for me to take stock. Life was showing me the importance of names, and of our links to our ancestors. Amazed by the similarities between these stories, I began to see myself as an invisible thread linking these two families via Barcelona and these children who were mediums.

It rained all night, and by the next morning the grass and earth were waterlogged. I felt like a walking sponge. Suddenly, a frightened deer shot out of the trees ten metres in front of me and ran off, closely followed by a pack of dogs. Three men with guns emerged from the wood in the distance and I realised they were hunters. Feeling sorry for the deer, and fearing stray bullets, I began to sing loudly as I walked. I was belting out a song by France Gall when I bumped into two surprised-looking hunters. 'It'll keep on raining whether I sing or not,' I said, shrugging my shoulders.

I arrived at Bourriot-Bergonce in a pretty bad mood, feeling like a hunted animal. I was sick of jumping every time I heard a gunshot. It was three in the afternoon, and I called the owner of the place I was due to stay because the address wasn't clear. He told me in no uncertain terms that it was too early and I should come back in two hours. I sank down on the ground, soaking my trousers in the process, but the sun took pity on me and came out at last. I was tired, wet through, and cross: I'd been on edge all day, and this man had just reflected all my negative energy back in my face, proving once again the importance of positive thoughts. I didn't realise that at the time, though, and simply thought to myself grumpily that my host, whose home in the middle of nowhere relied on walkers like me for trade, was rather lacking in business sense.

As I sat slumped by the side of the road, tipping out brown water from my sodden boots, I saw a man with a huge rucksack walking in my direction. We got talking, and I learned that his name was Bernard, he was retired, and he was following the same route – but each of his stages was forty-two kilometres! We were booked into the same place, so he sat down next to me to wait. He mentioned that he'd accidentally stepped in a hole that morning, and had begun to feel **sciatica** coming on. I asked what he'd been thinking about when it happened, and he thought for a moment and said he'd been feeling angry with two Dutch men who hadn't wanted to share a meal with him the previous evening, or even talk to him, even though they spoke French. I described the five wounds, and asked which one best described his experience. He chose rejection, and I explained that the benevolent universe had selected this wound and that he was attracting people and situations that would give him the chance to be healed. The idea resonated with him, so I suggested that he should thank the Dutch men, and even the hole in the road, and then try to identify the *original* rejection in his child-hood in order to cleanse the ties of suffering with his father or mother. 'Nobody has ever explained things so clearly before,' he said. The next day he was free of pain, and set off on the next stage after the best night's sleep he'd had in a long time.

The grandmother who was my host at the next hostel offered me a peach Armagnac aperitif to 'help me dry off', and our conversation soon turned to the invisible. When she and her husband had bought this property, they had discussed the fact that the barn hadn't been built in the right place. A week later a storm passed over, and lightning struck the barn, burning it to the ground. 'With the insurance money we were able to rebuild the barn in a better place. I've always thought that some benevolent being heard our conversation and the weather decided to do us a favour. It happened so quickly,' she said. As I listened to her, I thought about the guardian of their house, who had sensed their benevolence and decided to give them a hand. Then I wondered: how should I interpret this endless rain along my route? The only benefit I'd got was a little notoriety, after I posted a photo of myself on Facebook wrapped in three yellow bin bags (my waterproof poncho having given up the ghost) with a caption explaining that I was modelling the latest autumn–winter trend.

At the next hostel in Eauze I met a French woman called Isabelle and a couple from Hamburg, Christopher and Maria. They guessed from the number of phone calls I was receiving that it was my birthday, and prepared a meal for me in celebration. Happy not to be eating alone, I quickly cancelled my restaurant reservation, and Isabelle and I hurried to the shop to buy a melon, pâté, two baguettes, some grapes and wine. As we ate, we introduced ourselves. Isabelle was a nurse in Limoges, Christopher was an HR manager in a hospital for people with physical disabilities, and Maria was a minister. We exchanged stories, and I told them about the ghosts of Raphael's uncle and Eleanor's grandmother. Isabelle told us that her father had a passion for homing pigeons: 'After he died, we had to empty his house so we could sell it, and the day I arrived there I saw a pigeon on the roof looking at me strangely. I thought of my father but didn't say anything. Later, my sister visited the house and she also saw the pigeon. When we returned together, we talked about it: "Did you see it too?" We decided to talk to it: "Dad, is that you, sending us a sign with this pigeon?" The bird looked at both of us and flew off. As though it was satisfied that we had understood. We never saw it again. But I still needed some convincing, so I said: "Dad, if it was you, I want to see a pigeon every day for the rest of my life." And I have, every day since then.' Every day for the next few days Isabelle sent me photos of pigeons she'd seen in the forest, whereas I hardly saw any.

Christopher was next, telling us that every time there was a problem with a staff member or patient at the hospital he would call on former colleagues who had died. He asked them for help, and things were always resolved quickly. An HR manager calling on ghosts to help him – not something you hear about every day! He added that one day, when his first wife was pregnant, they put the new pram next to a window in one of the bedrooms. A pigeon immediately came and perched on the sill, staying there for several days until the baby was born. As soon as the baby was placed in the pram, the bird flew off. They gave their child a name that means *dove, symbol of peace.*

Maria looked at me. 'What about you?' she asked.

'I am making this journey as a tribute to my grandmother, and her name was Maria.'

As I said this, I realised that the two shared a name. It was unbelievable. What were the chances that two out of four people should tell a strange story involving a pigeon, and the two others should share a strong connection to the name Maria? We were strangers and yet I had the feeling we were linked.

After my birthday, the sun began to shine more consistently. The sky must have seen how much I was in need of drying out, and duly sent the clouds elsewhere. The next day I met a farmer along my route; his name was Christian and he told me he made a habit of offering tea to passing walkers. I thanked him, saying that this welcome hot drink on a cool morning was like a birthday present for me. He replied that it was his birthday that day. A special shared moment.

Françoise, whom I stayed with three days later, shared my birthday. Life weaves a cloth of threads that are invisible but real nonetheless.

At Vic-en-Bigorre I made an appointment with a massage therapist who agreed to see me at 6 p.m. even though that was her official closing time. She ended up giving me a massage that lasted an hour and a half – my body clearly needed it! She was suffering from carpal tunnel pain in her wrist, and I offered to explain the symbolism of this problem. She agreed, and I told her that it can mean that we're unable to stand up to what someone is telling us. She admitted that she had been the target of manipulative abuse by her ex-husband. I had written a book on precisely this subject three months earlier, and was able to give her some advice.

Further on I met the abbot at the Abbey of Tarasteix, who, for a ridiculously low price, offered me accommodation, dinner and breakfast. When he learned of my love of nature, he showed me around this wonderful site, where centuries-old olive trees flourish alongside rare species. I decided to interview him for *Inexploré* magazine and he rounded off the day with a short organ recital, not knowing that the organ has always been my favourite instrument, ever since my other grandmother used to play it when I was young.

Philippe, someone I'd never met but who works at the sanctuary in Lourdes, had been following my progress on Facebook and generously offered to be my guide when I arrived. I told him that after reading my posts, several people with reduced mobility had told me that they felt as though they'd been walking alongside me towards this sacred place. He held out the 10-litre container he'd been holding, saying: 'This is for you, so you won't have to walk even further to buy one, and you can fill it with holy water from Lourdes. I was going to give it to some friends this evening but I'll give them your story instead.'

This journey was an exchange of energies. Connections between living beings appeared before my eyes thanks to these myriad synchronicities: a series of apparently unconnected events that *chance* assembled along my path.

When we meet other people . . . we meet ourselves.

We don't necessarily need to go for a long walk to unburden ourselves of our old anger and resentment. Meditation, swimming, gardening, a short walk . . . almost any activity will do, enabling us to change profoundly. As we walk, we pick up energy from plants. As we breathe deeply, we allow our molecules to regenerate and thus expel old wounds. Nature is overflowing with positive waves. In summer we can even walk barefoot in order to heighten our sensations and our proximity to the nourishing earth. By looking after ourselves, we allow our light to shine on others and connect ourselves to the universe.

Conclusion

Together we have explored a new way of looking at life, and examined the challenging scenarios that can lie concealed behind failure and illness. The path you have walked will reconnect you with your body. You are now able to communicate with it as you would with a close friend, and restore its healing powers. You are now in touch with the secrets of your soul, which whispers that healing your wounds is the great challenge that you accepted before your birth. You also know that adversity, ordeals and frustrations are so many messages from the universe, helping you to rebuild yourself completely. These tools are now yours, and grant you access to immense serenity. Some recurrent problems will even disappear, and, when difficulties do arise, you will be surprised by your ability to effect a change in attitude that turns every ordeal into an experience. You will instantly remember that something positive is trying to break through. After all, don't we have to put 'muck' on our roses if we want them to grow tall and strong? You'll look for the wound rooted in your past that keeps replaying itself, perhaps a failure inherited from your parents, grandparents, or even more remote ancestors who shared your name. By practising these techniques you will rid yourself of the emotional earthquake and its recent aftershocks. You'll no longer place the blame on other people, microbes, viruses, bad lack or other external forces. Isn't it wonderful to know that the solution is within you, and that, by changing your perspective, you have the power to shed your burdens forever?

You have gained powerful allies in the form of invisible forces all around you. They will talk to you through dreams. The only challenge now is to set aside the voice in your mind saying that only what is visible exists, and to learn to ask for this unusual form of help at any time. When you have experienced the power of their aid several times, you will no longer be in any doubt. Your reconnection with the intangible will allow them to care for you, and you will find yourself thanking them several times each day, in the sure knowledge that they have come to your aid.

You will have understood as you read this book that nothing magical is at work here. It is your own journey towards the secret power of forgiveness that is the ultimate key to your liberation. This forgiveness is a flow of renewal capable of washing away old ordeals and severe illness. Every day, resentment will recede and forgiveness will grow within you. Sustained by a profound and sincere intention, you will walk towards a new vitality and confident wellbeing. That is the key to your energy. Your life is already changing for the better.

WHAT TO DO IN THE CASE OF ILLNESS

1. You have fallen ill: this is an opportunity to understand the message your body is sending you via your symptoms.

2. First, consult a doctor and take any medication needed.

3. Study the information that your body, your best ally, is sending you. Try to identify the painful event that sparked this illness. Ask yourself the questions in technique 2. Whom did you see and what did you hear just before falling ill? If necessary, use the symbolism of diseases from page 44 to 50 to help you. If you can't find anything, practise techniques 10 and 11 in order to make contact with your guide. Before going to bed, ask your guide to enlighten you through your dreams.

4. Carry out technique 3 and speak to your body several times every day. Speaking out loud with **energy**, express your will to get well, addressing the 99 per cent of yourself that relates to your energy. For example, you can say: '**Thank you, body. I have now understood that this emotional problem is at the root of my illness. You can remove the symptoms of [. . .] because I am going to work to cleanse this emotion by practising various techniques.**'

5. Visualise the cleansing of the pain, imagining that you are expelling it with your breath as described in technique 4.

6. Carry out technique 5 first, then a soul recovery (technique 6) in relation to anyone whose attitude has

destabilised you, and who has taken your energy. In order to rebuild yourself in a way that lasts, you need to be *whole*.

7. Think about the emotional wound (injustice, rejection, abandonment, humiliation, betrayal) revealed by this illness. It is the echo of another (more serious) wound that occurred during your childhood, or that you have inherited from your ancestors.

8. Cleanse or cut the ties of suffering (techniques 7 or 8) with the people associated with these inherited emotional burdens.

9. You have drawn these people or events towards you in order to heal the effects of the original upheaval. One day, you will manage to forgive them, and even thank them for having allowed you to transform yourself.

10. Taking as much time as you need, forgive yourself (your soul) for having set yourself so many challenges before being incarnated.

11. Repeat steps 3 to 5 every day until your symptoms disappear. You should also repeat techniques 5, 6 and 7 or 8, but wait **at least** a fortnight between sessions to allow your body time to integrate the new energies. Give yourself the time you need to heal. As you complete each stage of these techniques, you can occasionally include other purification rituals such as putting down roots and bed cleansing.

WHAT TO DO IN THE CASE OF AN ORDEAL

1. Going through a difficult experience is an opportunity to repair an old wound.

2. Express your feelings out loud to yourself: your anger, fear, shame, frustration, hatred or sadness.

3. Express your feelings (whatever they may be) towards the other person concerned.

4. Identify the wound: betrayal, injustice, rejection, humiliation or abandonment. If you can't identify one, practise techniques 10 and 11 to make contact with your guide. Before going to bed, ask your guide to enlighten you through your dreams.

5. Don't make yourself or those around you suffer the effects of this wound.

6. We have all been through difficult times. Practise technique 5 (soul recovery) to prevent yourself losing any further energy. If you feel overwhelmed by someone's attitude towards you (their silences, their contradictions, their endless criticisms or reproaches), it means that you're losing energy and this person is feeding off it. Practise technique 6 in relation to them. Ask yourself whether your parents, grandparents, siblings, uncles or aunts might also have taken your energy (without meaning to), causing you to be constantly destabilised. Practise technique 6 with the people in question.

   Note: If you are being mistreated at work, by people you know, or by your partner, it is absolute proof that

you have lost part of your energy. Carry out technique 5
first and then 6 in relation to these people.

7. Cleanse or cut the ties of suffering (techniques 7 or 8)
with the people linked to these painful emotions.

8. Observe the cycles repeating themselves and cleanse (or
cut) the ties of suffering with the family members at the
origin of these inherited personal upheavals.

9. Reconnect with your inner child (using technique 9) in
order to remove the feelings of guilt at the origins of
your fears and blockages, which began in childhood.

10. You have drawn these people or events towards you in
order to heal the effects of the original upheaval. Taking
as much time as you need, forgive them, so that one
day you will be able to thank them for the person you
have become.

11. Forgive yourself (your soul) for having set yourself so
many challenges before being incarnated.

12. Repeat techniques 5, 6 and 7 or 8, but wait **at least** a
fortnight between sessions to allow your body time to
integrate the new energies. Give yourself the time you
need to heal. If you need to carry out these techniques
in relation to a large number of people, do them in
groups of three or six at a time, leaving at least a
fortnight between each session.

If a painful emotion is reactivated, it means that there is
something remaining to be cleansed. Ask your guide to
enlighten you through your dreams, or to suggest a

therapist who will help you to see this ordeal more clearly. As you complete each stage of these techniques, you can occasionally include other purification rituals such as putting down roots and bed cleansing.

Acknowledgements

This book has grown out of the invaluable advice I have received from others, and from the sometimes challenging practices that life has offered to me as a means of rebuilding myself. I would therefore like to thank all the healers, mediums and shamans who have been generous enough to share their experience and techniques with me. The time has come to spread this knowledge more widely, so this book is a crucible, a repository of all the forgotten knowledge that I spent almost ten years collecting, trying out, and often adapting.

I also owe a debt of thanks to the doctors, psychiatrists and psychotherapists who have contributed their skills to this book. First, to the psychotherapist Jacques Roques, co-founder of the EMDR France association and creator of psychoneurobiology, for having allowed me to include an important idea concerning guilt, but also for the parallel between soul recovery and the 'light stream' technique, and for having given me permission to state my conclusion that we can work out that there is a million times more energy and information in our bodies than matter. To the psychiatrist Jean Sandretto for the opportunity to discuss the all-important idea of the mirror neuron. To the doctor and osteopath Patrick Jouhaud, who teaches the dynamic of living systems in paediatric osteopathy, and who suggested that I draw on the idea of synchronicity in the chapter 'Upgrade Your Life'. To Dr Gérard Ostermann, a psychotherapist and professor of medicine, for having drawn my attention to the essential fact that an emotion is never negative, because it carries information about how to rebuild ourselves. Thank you to all these for having shown me that the symbolism of disease is simply a collection of statistics, and that the best way of identifying the event that sparked an illness is to seek the painful ordeal at its origin.

A huge thank you to my precious friends: to Natalie Fuchs for her unwavering support and for putting me in touch with someone who changed my life by introducing me to a new technique; to Nathalie Lenseigne, who encouraged me to stop hiding behind writing novels and show my true nature; to Laurie Fatovic for listening, and for having helped me to conceive the idea of this book; to Florence Hubert for her connections and compassionate presence, especially after my sister's death; to Loan Miège for her generosity and help on numerous occasions; to Marie-Pierre Dillenseger for her excellent advice and for being by my side when I had the life-changing MRI scan that diagnosed my double slipped disc; to Bénédicte Touchard de Morant, endlessly supportive for over thirty years – I'll never forget your phone call and your questions just as I was revising this book one final time, helping me to make some vital final adjustments.

Endless thanks to all of you who have attended my workshops or lectures, and have written to me to tell me about being healed, about feeling that your lives have improved, and sometimes even about little miracles. Your transformations are precious gifts, and an unending source of encouragement.

Thank you also to The Boss, Francis Esménard, who has a knack for being discreetly and yet powerfully supportive, to the CEO of Albin Michel, Gilles Haéri, for his enthusiasm when I first spoke to him about this project, and especially to my editor Lise Boëll for her instinctive genius for bringing out the best in me, as well as to Estelle Cerutti, Damien Bergeret, Iris Néron-Bancel and Florence Le Grand, whose questions and suggestions

THE KEY TO YOUR ENERGY

helped me to express my ideas. This book has gained a lot from this dream team.

Infinite thanks to my parents, my sisters and my family, for the person I have become. Thank you to my son, whom I love so dearly for his pure heart, his sensitivity and his outlook on life. Thank you to my husband for the special bond we share, for his patience when things weren't going well for me, his respect for my work, his love, and his constant kind esteem, which helps me to continue along my path.

Thank you to A. L. forever.